NEGOTIATE

NEGOTIATE

Willem Mastenbroek

Basil Blackwell

Copyright © Willem Mastenbroek 1989

First published as *Onderhandelen* by Spectrum Uitgeverij Het, BV, Amsterdam 1984

This translation first published in 1989

Basil Blackwell Ltd
108 Cowley Road, Oxford, OX4 1JF, UK

Basil Blackwell Inc.
432 Park Avenue South, Suite 1503
New York, NY 10016, USA

British Library Cataloguing in Publication Data
Mastenbroek, Willem F. G.
  Negotiate.
  1. Management. Negotiation
  I. Title
  658.4′5
  ISBN 0-631-16348-4

Library of Congress Cataloging in Publication Data
Mastenbroek, W. F. G.
  Negotiate/Willem Mastenbroek.
    p.   cm.
  Bibliography: p.
  Includes index.
  ISBN 0-631-16348-4
  1. Negotiate in business.   I. Title.
HD58.6.M375   1989
658.4-dc19   88-37656
       CIP

Typeset in 11 on 13 pt Sabon
by Joshua Associates Ltd, Oxford
Printed in Great Britain by
T. J. Press, Padstow, Cornwall

Contents

Preface

As a consultant I initially became interested in negotiating as a practical way of dealing with different interests; as a social scientist I was puzzled by the separate findings about and insights into the process of negotiating. My subsequent interest in developing integrative frameworks and models were the sources of inspiration for this book.

As an organizational consultant, I have taken part in a large number of discussions and meetings in a great many organizations. Although it never occurred to anyone to call these meetings negotiations, that was precisely what they were. Some of them were conducted so clumsily that deadlock threatened; or the situation deteriorated into covert or more open hostility – a development often not only unintended but also unnecessary. These experiences have made it clear to me that negotiating skills have a prominent and constructive role to play. I have also seen how quickly people pick things up in this field. Negotiating is a type of behaviour which everyone meets, and practises, every day. Whether we want to or not, whether we realize it or not, we all negotiate.

With this in mind, it never fails to amaze me how maladroitly people sometimes go about their 'negotiating'. For example, they

- confuse negotiating with scoring points;
- neglect the climate ('let's get down to business');
- overlook the fact that their relationship with their 'constituency' is a negotiating relation;

- think negotiations have failed when matters reach an impasse;
- confuse tenacious negotiating with obstinacy;
- are blind to their negotiating style and its effects on others;
- fail to recognize manipulations both of themselves and of others;
- see adjournments as a sign of weakness;
- have no idea how they physically sit and what sort of non-verbal behaviour they exhibit;
- view a joint search for solutions as giving in.

It is equally surprising to see how fast people can learn on these points. That is what has encouraged me to publish my work on negotiating in the form of this book.

This book could never have come into being without the inspiration of others. I wish particularly to thank here two colleagues at the Holland Consulting Group, Pieter Jan van Delden and Gerco Ezerman, for their suggestions; also Mrs Carol Stennes for her work in translating the Dutch text into English. Gillian Bromley, Basil Blackwell copy-editor, did a thorough job in preparing the English edition. Her work enhanced the accessibility of the text considerably. Great thanks are also due to clients. It was they who confronted me with a very wide variety of negotiating problems and experiences. Their persistence in making critical remarks and creative suggestions helped to bring this work to its final form.

PART I

Introduction

CHAPTER 1

Background and Structure

1.1 Background

The negotiating model described in the following chapters has grown over ten years and has its origins in my work as an organizational consultant. Many organizational problems have negotiating aspects. An organization is composed of interdependent units each of which has interests of its own. Every important decision in organizations involves some degree of contention between the parties involved. Strategy formulation, cutbacks, the allocation of personnel, budgets, authority, important projects, space in buildings, provision of secretarial support, automation facilities – all of these are issues in which negotiating plays a role.

Recent developments in organizations have strengthened the need for constructive negotiation. I am referring to prevalent tendencies towards decentralization, smaller and more autonomous units, a stronger market orientation, a more entrepreneurial climate. Organizational units are thrown back more and more upon their own resources. Less intervention from higher levels in the organization goes hand in hand with stronger rivalries between units on comparable levels. This tendency towards both greater autonomy and greater responsibility calls for the capacity to negotiate with 'rival' interests inside and outside the organization.

I have gradually come to see negotiating as a skill that can successfully combine the pursuit of self-interest with the fact of interdependence. More than that, negotiating can even increase the value of interdependence in the sense that people learn better how to take advantage of it.

My interest in negotiating having been aroused, it turned out to be no easy matter to find out what good negotiating was. The literature proved not to be of much help. The more practical works were basically lists of tactical rules of thumb, and although they made fascinating reading, soon I could not see the wood for the trees. The more scientific literature, some 400–500 detailed studies, lacked both integration and any clear relationship to practical problems. There were also some attempts to formulate fairly abstract models. I realized that more research and more practical work would be needed if truly useful material were to be written.

My first presentations and articles on negotiating provoked all kinds of reactions: the number of responses and questions from a wide range of organizations was an enormous encouragement. These expressions of interest brought me into contact with a wide variety of negotiators: diplomats, executives, personnel managers, bankers, officials of associations and commodity traders, to name only some. My own consulting work also made ever clearer the need to develop skills that would do justice to *both* mutual dependency *and* self-interest in interpersonal relations.

Ultimately, the following three steps led to the model of negotiating described in this book.

1 From my study of the existing literature, I selected four perspectives which seemed to open the way to a better understanding of negotiating:

a Negotiating as a set of *tactical rules of thumb*. There are a great many of these dos and don'ts, all of which make up interesting and useful material, but material that needs to be set within a structuring framework. This book develops such a framework.
b Negotiating as a skill based on the handling of a number of *dilemmas*. Material on this is spread throughout the literature. This is a perspective that I have worked out in more detail.
c Negotiating as a *process* with a structure in time. There is a great deal of material on this, which, with a few adjustments, was quite useful.
d Negotiating as a complex of different *types of activities*. One classic study (Walton and McKersie, 1965) is based on this

perspective. The basic principle has been incorporated here, but a largely different typology of basic activities has been developed.

2 This material was further developed over the years. A primary concern was that the concepts and principles employed should be more easily recognized, identified and applied. Through systematic interviews and group discussions with experienced negotiators, and numerous conferences involving widely divergent types of negotiators, the original material gained form and coherence. Concepts that were difficult to recognize disappeared, as did insights which were considered to be of little practical value. The knowledge and experience of competent negotiators, and their challenging questions and critical remarks, made it clear that improvements and adaptations were both possible and desirable. For example, the original list of twelve negotiating dilemmas has been whittled down to four, and all those four have been drastically reformulated.

A second important challenge was to integrate the material, the diversity of which was at first a handicap. It was unsystematic and lacked internal consistency: the various perspectives remained separate. Together the corpus was simply too complicated. To make it easier to handle, I had to work out the material in the following manner.

- The basic concepts had to be as few as possible.
- These concepts had to order a complex of behaviours and problems into certain patterns: they had to offer an orientation, such as, for example, the phase structure of negotiations, or the 'cooperation–negotiation–fighting' continuum. These and other concepts describe characteristics of interpersonal relations and the ways in which people deal with them.
- The concepts had to relate as directly as possible to the actual behaviour of negotiators.
- The concepts had to form an integrative model.

3 Only a transparent and compact construct can both offer an orientation and grip of actual negotiating situations. Step by step, the material was developed towards this end. One could hardly call the process a logical one; it was more a case of trial and error. Variants were developed and tried out, sometimes on the basis of experiences and observations, sometimes in discussions with experts,

sometimes during conferences. A series of simulations of 'real' negotiation experiences outlined more and more clearly the notions about the essential 'levers'. Direct feedback on these ideas served to show how realistic they were. The direction in which I was looking may have been clear, but it was a matter of probing. Gradually, a transparent and workable model emerged, constructed around two basic dimensions of social behaviour:

1 the cooperating–fighting dimension;
2 the exploring–avoiding dimension.

These two dimensions have their foundations in a structural factor: *interdependence*. The inevitable choices on both dimensions are influenced by the nature of that interdependence, or rather by the balance of power between the parties. Together these two dimensions show the possible ways of coping with various forms of interdependence.

The first dimension coordinates and integrates the most important *dilemmas* and *types of activities* in negotiating. The second dimension covers the *phases* of the negotiating process and the related *procedures* which parties can use.

This model not only enables negotiations to be better described and better understood; it also provides numerous indications of how to negotiate effectively. In addition, it has a bearing on a wide range of particular facets of negotiating, such as preparing negotiations, personal negotiating styles and chairing negotiations.

1.2 Structure

Part II of this book (chapters 2–8) explains an *integrative model of negotiating*. A summary of the model may be found in chapter 8, which is written in such a way as to be self-contained; the reader may begin with this chapter to gain acquaintance with the model, the component parts of which are dealt with in chapters 2–7.

The model described in part II is applicable to many different types of negotiations. One type, negotiating inside organizations, is treated specifically in chapter 16, where negotiating is linked to a particular type of organizational structure that can improve motivation and promote an entrepreneurial spirit among employees.

Part III discusses a number of special problems and situations.

These are questions with which I have been confronted so often over the years that I felt compelled to explore them in detail. They include preparing negotiations, negotiating from a dependent position, personal negotiating styles, and chairing negotiations.

Appendix 1 contains a survey of the literature, identifying the most important schools of thought. By now, the literature has become quite extensive. To give the reader an idea of the various perspectives, I have classified these works and added some commentary about each type.

Negotiating is a skill we learn primarily by practising it; hence the inclusion of the training material in appendix 2. Several exercises appear here, involving role-playing and simulations; to make them more effective, an indication is given of which aspect of negotiating each exercise helps clarify. As an additional aid various evaluation forms and summaries are presented.

Throughout the book I have tried to present my ideas as clearly as possible with extensive use of tables and diagrams which invite the reader to classify and evaluate his own behaviour and that of possible opponents, and in addition serve as summaries to facilitate rapid comprehension and easy application.

Finally, I should note that for the sake of consistency and simplicity I have used the masculine personal pronoun throughout the text. This is to be understood to include negotiators – and other persons – of both sexes.

PART II

A Model of Negotiating

CHAPTER 2

Negotiating: An Orientation

Relations between negotiators show the following characteristics:

- the parties are interdependent;
- they also have different interests;
- there is not a vast difference in power.

How can we deal with such situations? Less and less by control from above, with power structures, formal hierarchies and accepted authority often no longer in the places they once held. Neither the harmony nor the conflict model is applicable in these situations. A model of mild confrontation or, more precisely, a negotiating model, is better. Why? Because negotiating is a combination of defending one's interests and doing justice to the interdependence. It is an alternative between cooperative and fighting behaviour; more than this, it is a discrete and separate social skill, quite distinct from other skills such as cooperating and fighting.

Cooperation is appropriate among people sharing similar interests and goals. It is the obvious solution if the benefits for those involved depend directly on the extent to which they can pool their resources: i.e. in a situation of strong interdependence.

Negotiating is the proper strategy in a case involving different, sometimes even competing interests, but where at the same time the two parties are interdependent to the degree that an agreement would yield advantages for both of them. The parties disagree, but they would like to arrive at an agreement, because both letting things drift and fighting are disadvantageous for both of them.

Fighting is the most likely strategy when, in the case of opposed interests, one party thinks it stands to gain more by fighting than by negotiating. Sometimes it is adopted as a strategy to gain recognition as a serious negotiating partner. A fighting strategy is concerned with influencing the balance of power. One party tries to reduce the opponent to submission, while taking all possible opportunities to strengthen its own power position.

The boundaries between these three approaches are not clear-cut. We might usefully think of them as a continuum. The more manifest the interdependency, the greater the chance of cooperative behaviour. Table 2.1 serves to clarify the three strategies.

Negotiating situations sometimes present difficult decisions because of the combination of self-interest and mutual dependency. Too often people are blind to anything but their own manifest interests, and this makes them opt for a harder strategy than is in

Table 2.1 Tactics used in cooperation, negotiation and fighting

Cooperation	Negotiation	Fighting
Conflict is seen as a common problem	Conflict is seen as a clash between different but mutually dependent interests	Conflict is seen as a question of 'winning or losing', 'over or under', 'we or they'
People present their own goals as accurately as possible	People exaggerate their own interests but pay attention to possible areas of agreement	People emphasize the superiority of their own objectives
Weak points and personal problems can be openly discussed	Personal problems are disguised or presented very circumspectly	Personal problems are treated as if they do not exist
The information provided is honest	The information given is not false, but one-sided. The facts favourable to one's own position are deliberately emphasized	If it can help to make the opponent submit, false information is deliberately spread
Discussion subjects are presented in terms of underlying problems	Agenda items are formulated in terms of alternative solutions	Points of disagreement are formulated in terms of one's own solution

Cooperation	Negotiation	Fighting
Possible solutions are tested against their practical consequences	Occasionally the linking of solutions to principles is used to put some pressure on the other side	One's own solutions are not only 'right', but they are rigidly tied to higher principles
Speaking out for one particular solution is deliberately delayed as long as possible	Strong preference for a particular solution is shown, but margins and concessions are taken for granted	An absolute and unconditional preference for one's own solution is expressed at every opportunity
Threats, confusion and taking advantage of the mistakes of others are seen as detrimental	Occasionally a modest and carefully calculated use is made of threats, confusion and surprise	Threats, confusion, shock effects, etc. may be used at any time to reduce the opponent to submission
Active participation of all parties concerned is encouraged	Contacts between parties are limited to only a few spokespersons	Contacts between the parties take place indirectly via 'declarations'
An attempt is made to spread power as much as possible and to let it play no further role	Power is occasionally tested, or attempts are made to influence the balance of power in one's own favour	Both parties engage in a permanent power struggle by strengthening their own organizations, increasing independence and dividing and isolating the opponent
People try to understand one another and share one another's personal concerns	Understanding the views of the other side is seen as a tactical instrument	No one bothers to understand the opponent
Personal irritations are expressed to clear the air of tensions that could hamper future cooperation	Personal irritations are suppressed or ventilated indirectly (e.g. with humour)	Irritations confirm negative and hostile images. Hostility is expressed to break down the other side
Both parties find it easy to call in outside expertise as an aid to decision-making	Third parties are brought in only if there is a complete deadlock	Outsiders are welcome only if they are 'blind' supporters

accordance with the strong interdependence. If they later discover that they have not foreseen the unfavourable consequences, so much mutual mistrust has been aroused that cooperation is almost impossible.

On the other hand, sometimes people opt too quickly for a cooperative strategy in situations which demand quite some caution about their own position. If attempts to cooperate do not have the expected effects, they feel disappointed and manipulated; there is then a strong tendency either to turn to fighting behaviour or to yield.

In the third place, it is remarkable how easily people allow themselves to be drawn into fighting behaviour, often by making reference to the 'less constructive behaviour' of the opponent. But the opponent sees it exactly the same way: and so the vicious circle is closed. Such processes, in which parties manoeuvre so clumsily that they become constricted in conflicts and struggles for prestige, are often spontaneous and, in a certain sense, unintentional. Looking back, the parties are dismayed to see themselves caught up in a spiral of growing hostilities. Insight into these 'spontaneous' dynamics and a large arsenal of behavioural alternatives can help prevent unwanted behavioural tendencies towards destructive conflicts. Negotiating skills have too long been neglected in this arsenal. To be able to take advantage of negotiating, it is important to see it as a type of activity which is appropriate to certain sorts of dependency relations, in which both conflict and cooperation have a place. In such cases, relying on cooperation alone can provoke a bitter struggle which will be hard to control.

Here lies what I like to call the paradox of cooperation: if, in situations involving contrasting interests, one decides to cooperate in openness and trust, one may actually increase the chance of a destructive conflict! There are examples in which a party thinks he can make negotiations take a smooth and amicable course by making a generous proposal at the outset. What happens is that the other party quickly rakes in its profits and then sits down to negotiate. Naturally, the negotiations become extremely arduous because one of the parties feels thoroughly deceived. And yet a negotiator hardly has an alternative in such a situation. Not only does he get the impression that there is more to be gained, but also life would otherwise be made difficult for him by a constituency which has been looking forward to talks in which their interests will be stoutly defended. The notion that if one adopts a cooperative attitude, the other side will do so as well, is untenable here. On the contrary, there is a tendency to see it as necessary yielding, or as weak and inept. It provokes exploitative and competitive behaviour; in the long run, it promotes resistance and revenge. So an attempt to apply a cooperative model in situations of contrasting interests can work out destructively.

We still seem to have a hard time grasping the fact that fighting and cooperation can be combined. Our thoughts and actions have long been dominated by a sharp distinction between harmony and conflict. And yet it is very possible to combine interdependence with a strong assertion of one's own interests. We could even say that such a combination gives relations a productive tension and vitality. Fighting and cooperation are to be seen as complementary. Negotiating involves a dynamic equilibrium between fighting and cooperation.

This balancing act between cooperation and fighting asks of us the capacity to deal with several dilemmas. 'Am I too open about my position or am I revealing too little?' 'To what extent should I trust the other party?' 'Would a sign of distrust harm the negotiating climate?' 'Must I be as tough as my constituency wants me to be, or should I show some understanding in order to increase the chance of a compromise?' Each of these questions illustrates the tensions between cooperation and fighting in a different way. Sometimes the dilemmas manifest themselves very vaguely as uncertainty and doubt, sometimes they appear explicitly in the awareness of a difficult choice. One is either too open or too closed, too tough or too compliant, too dominant or too modest, too cool or too friendly.

These dilemmas can be regarded as aspects of the polarity between cooperation and fighting. Each dilemma suggests a subtle equilibrium to be attained between too much or too little. A differentiated approach to this equilibrium implies tension and doubt. The temptation to lean toward one of these poles may be great: it may seem that to do so would make the situation much easier to handle. This is why skilled negotiators dislike having to deal with inexperienced opponents, because they are generally too incalculable. Before the limits of what is attainable on both sides have been explored, the novice may have an emotional outburst or, in all innocence, manoeuvre himself into a corner. A particular and real danger is the tendency to adopt an 'all or nothing', 'win or lose' attitude. This may happen without a person being aware of it himself: he adopts a 'point-scoring' attitude, becomes suspicious and starts to withhold more information than is necessary.

Negotiating is a matter of cautiously and flexibly dealing with several dilemmas. These dilemmas fit into an analysis of negotiating as a complex of five types of activities (see note at end of this chapter):

1 Obtaining *substantial results*, dividing the costs and benefits, achieving the goals dictated by your interests.
2 Influencing the *balance of power* between parties: keeping it in equilibrium or making it a little more favourable to oneself.
3 Influencing the *atmosphere*: promoting a constructive climate and positive personal relations.
4 Influencing the *constituency*: reinforcing one's own position with respect to the constituency on whose behalf one is negotiating.

These four activities show different underlying intentions and have different effects. All four are important at the negotiating table. Each of them will be treated separately in the chapters that follow. Each of these four activities is, in a different way, characterized by the tension between cooperation and fighting.

Finally, a fifth important activity is:

5 Influencing the *procedures*: developing procedures that allow people to be flexible while increasing the chances of reaching a favourable compromise.

This fifth activity is not characterized by the polarity between fighting and cooperation, but, as we will see, by the tension between exploring/active and avoiding/passive behaviour.

In chapter 8, 'Negotiating Effectively: Conclusions', the five activities will be integrated into a coordinating model.

Note

The pioneering work on negotiating as several types of activities is that of Walton and McKersie (1965). Walton and McKersie distinguished the activities of (1) distributive bargaining, directed at maximizing one's share of substantial benefits; (2) integrative bargaining, directed at problem-solving and the increase of mutual benefits; (3) attitudinal structuring; and (4) intra-organizational bargaining. The model presented here also distinguishes the latter two activities as activities 2 and 4. In my view, dealing with the power relations between the parties is of such central importance that it warrants a separate place in the model. I do not distinguish distributive and integrative bargaining as separate activities. Here they are integrated in the activities directed at obtaining substantial results. Finally, the 'binding element' of the four essential types of activities is: influencing the procedures.

It is fascinating to see how Walton and McKersie struggled with the 'mixed-motive' nature of negotiating: initially they divided negotiations into distributive and integrative activities, which had the nature of fighting and cooperating respectively. However, the mixed-motive nature of negotiating implies that it is simultaneously distributive and integrative; this mixture is so strong that the distinction cannot be maintained. Walton and McKersie thus introduced 'mixed bargaining'. They clearly recognized several of the dilemmas that play a role here and managed to describe quite pointedly the 'mixed' behaviour they entail. However, in a later study, Walton tried to 'eliminate' mixed negotiating by recommending separation of the distributive and integrative elements – e.g. by the agenda, another time, another place, other negotiators (Walton, 1972, p. 104).

Apart from the question of whether this is practicable, such an attempt clearly illustrates the difficulty that we evidently still have with the simultaneity of fighting and cooperation, of self-interest and interdependence. But, as we have repeatedly seen, this simultaneity and this 'mixed' nature are perfectly normal in negotiating situations. They involve a dynamic equilibrium between fighting and cooperation, not an either–or choice. This dynamic equilibrium shifts towards fighting or cooperation depending on the situation (degree of interdependence, divergence of interests, phase of the negotiations and personal styles). One characteristic remains: a constant balancing between the two poles.

CHAPTER 3

Obtaining Substantial Results

It is generally those aspects of negotiating which are aimed at achieving tangible results that receive the most attention. I am referring to activities which focus on the *content* of negotiations: arguments, facts, standpoints, goals, interests, basic assumptions, compromise proposals, concessions and conditions. Negotiators try to influence the distribution of costs and benefits in a way favourable to them in matters of content, for example

- by creating space to manoeuvre;
- by presenting their proposals as self-evident;
- by presenting facts favourable to themselves;
- by making only small concessions.

The most important activities are:

- a tactical exchange of *information* about goals, expectations and acceptable solutions;
- presenting one's *position* in a way that influences the other party's perception of what is attainable;
- working step by step towards a compromise with *concessions* made on both sides.

The tactical choices a negotiator must make here involve striking a balance between yielding and more persistent or even obstinate behaviour. Figure 3.1 illustrates this dilemma.

Coping with this dilemma can be greatly complicated by the fact

Figure 3.1 The 'conceding versus stubborn' dilemma

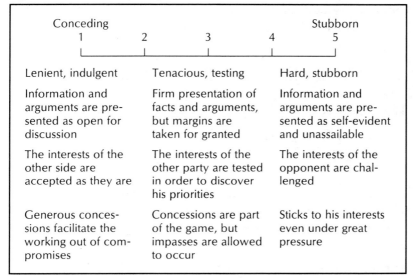

Conceding		Stubborn
1 2 3	4	5
Lenient, indulgent	Tenacious, testing	Hard, stubborn
Information and arguments are presented as open for discussion	Firm presentation of facts and arguments, but margins are taken for granted	Information and arguments are presented as self-evident and unassailable
The interests of the other side are accepted as they are	The interests of the other party are tested in order to discover his priorities	The interests of the opponent are challenged
Generous concessions facilitate the working out of compromises	Concessions are part of the game, but impasses are allowed to occur	Sticks to his interests even under great pressure

that a negotiator is often not yet certain what goals are realistically attainable. To gain this knowledge he must first find out more about the priorities and options open to the other side. In order to arrive at results, the parties must have information about each other's goals. The party with a head start in this is at an advantage. It is easier for its negotiator to determine a good strategy and a favourable starting position. He knows better what is attainable and so he knows how far he can go in his demands. This increases the chance that he will not have to go to extremes in his willingness to make concessions. Both parties will be aware of this, and it makes them cautious in revealing information. Both parties are also aware that keeping back too much makes effective negotiating impossible.

A second complicating factor in dealing with this dilemma is the tendency to keep the opponent's expectations low and to present one's own wishes as self-evident and unassailable. A negotiator knows that the resolution he demonstrates will have an influence, but he sees the determination of his opponent in the same light. Both of them know that margins are built in. They will have to show some acceptance of this if any results are to be achieved.

There are several ways of handling this dilemma. They will be treated here under three categories: tactical use of information, choice of position and concessions.

3.1 The tactical use of information

The tactical exchange of information has two purposes:

1 to find the opponent's bottom offer and bring it down further;
2 to clarify one's own demands in such a way that the opponent will see them as realistic and inevitable.

In a nutshell, we are concerned here with *influencing the 'attainabilities'*.

Tactical information can be provided in several ways. They include:

- Information that boils down to 'it will also hurt the opponent'. The union may say: 'If company headquarters are moved to Birmingham, at least a quarter of the staff will decide to look for new jobs. And it is precisely the best qualified employees who will have the easiest time finding them.'
- Information in which a concession is inflated in the hope that one will thus not have to make any further concessions. Management may say: 'Dropping the annual vacation closedown costs the company millions. You will understand that this is really a very big concession on our part.'
- Providing information by choosing examples selectively. Management again may say: 'You want mediators in all departments. A similar system was introduced in Holland and the results were disastrous.'

Providing tactical information is a party's right. But it will be effective only if the assertions can be substantiated with facts or by sources that also have some authority for the opponent. If negotiators seldom or never succeed in this, they become mere caricatures and lose their credibility. The border between tactical and incorrect information is rather vague. Providing patently false information generally has the effect of weakening one's own negotiating position and considerably worsening the relationship between the parties. Interpreting and providing information in a light favourable to yourself is considered normal; the relationship need not suffer from it at all.

These are fairly mild tactics to influence interests and positions. To test the opponent's position there are also harder tactics, for example:

- Adjourning or breaking off negotiations.
- Ignoring the choice of position of the other party.
- Setting a time limit (a variant is continuing the meeting into the night).
- Referring to the constituency: 'I can't sell this to my people.'
- Referring to personal consequences: 'If this is the way it has to be, I quit.'
- Setting an ultimatum.
- Bluffing – for example, by not showing any interest; or, if a demand is not accepted, by raising it at a following opportunity. There is a chance that the other party then asks you to be 'reasonable'; that is, they show that they are prepared to talk about the first demand. A variant is starting out by being reasonable, but making new stipulations just when the opponent has accepted the previous ones. Regular use of this ploy to obtain extra concessions is known as 'salami tactics'.
- Sending a spokesperson. The person with real authority makes sure that he is not present at the negotiations. He sends a representative and then calmly sits back to see what direction the negotiations will take. In this way he keeps his hands free and commits himself to nothing. The other party can only defend itself by immediately bringing up the opponent's level of authority, and, if they feel this is not satisfactory, by demanding to negotiate with the man who can make decisions.
- The good and the evil negotiator. Sometimes a negotiating team makes use of a well-known interrogation technique. One of them takes the hard line, to the point of being unreasonable, while the other one is quite rational. A party will then try to do business with the 'good' one, whose 'reasonable' position can turn out to be fairly substantial after all.

These tactics must be used with care. If they give the impression that the situation is defined as a fighting situation, then the chance of destructive escalation increases. They must stand in proportion to the importance of the matter. You must know how to *dose* them: they are only effective if they are not used too much. Then, when they are used, they are accepted as a way of exploring the limits of what tangible results can be reached. A negotiator who makes too much use of them will get the reputation of being wilful and aggressive, and may lose his credibility.

3.2 Choosing a position

In general it is good to start negotiating with an exchange of information on interests and priorities. *Do not choose a position too early by presenting your proposal, solution or choice!*

We must distinguish between the tactic of a closed position and that of an open position.

3.2.1 CLOSED POSITION

The tactic of the closed position has several variants:

- 'take it or leave it';
- the ultimatum;
- the *fait accompli*;
- final offer first.

The last one is the toughest variant. It implies that one of the parties presents his proposals as final and as really the last word right away at the outset of the negotiations. Such a tactic has a few very clear advantages. One party takes the initiative and forces the other on to the defensive. One party places responsibility for a possible breakdown in the negotiations with the other party. Furthermore, immediately choosing a position creates a reputation of resolute seriousness and credibility. This can be very important for future negotiations. But it also involves considerable risk. It makes it very hard to go back without a serious loss of face, even if it later appears that some things have been overlooked. Particularly if the negotiating relationship is poor, the other party will feel it has no choice, and this in itself can arouse much resistance.

This tactic has its best chance of succeeding when one knows precisely where the bottom line lies for the opponent. Then an extra concession can often be won, because the other party does not want to run the risk that negotiations are broken off over that single issue.

3.2.2 OPEN POSITION

Parties often enter into negotiations with an open position, perhaps making statements about their own interests and about their own view of what is to be done, but leaving the maximum room for manoeuvre. Sometimes one opens with an extreme position while stating that one is prepared to be flexible. If the opening choices are very unrealistic, this tactic is also known as 'blue-sky bargaining'. Generally speaking, this is not very sensible because it can erode credibility, and is felt to be opportunistic. If a position really must be taken, it is generally best to start with 'the highest defensible claim'. This implies that the negotiator can substantiate his claims and that he has created room to manoeuvre.

Gradually more information about the opponent's position is revealed and one's own choice of position can become firmer. The negotiators keep concessions in reserve so that, if the discussions reach a deadlock, they can be set in motion again with a small concession or by making an exchange at a certain point.

Important *advantages* of this method are:

- parties are not entirely dependent on advance information;
- an atmosphere of give and take is created; the relationship is not likely to deteriorate;
- the risk involved in leaving a position occupied earlier is not as great; the danger of pinning oneself down to an untenable position becomes smaller.

A *disadvantage* is that the chance to influence the other party in its choice of position becomes smaller. To compensate for this as much as possible, the information-giving/seeking tactics described above may be used. Another *disadvantage* is that, by continually making concessions, a party somewhat discredits each new choice of position in advance. Such a manner of negotiating can be rather frustrating for the participants, because they may feel they suffer a slight loss of face with each concession.

3.3 Concessions

After the exploratory phase, and once various proposals have been presented, the usual course is to make small concessions and to make sure that you get something in return. Some negotiators are extremely adroit at referring in passing to a possible concession. As soon as they notice that they will not get what they expected in return, they immediately withdraw the concession or even flatly deny that they ever considered making it.

In order to obtain concessions, it is important to specify what you want of the other party. Questions like: 'Can't the other side meet us halfway?' or 'Is that all you can do?', rather than leading to concessions, only produce lengthy explanations of why this is, unfortunately, as far as they can go. It puts the other side on the defensive, just as the buyer of a second-hand car who asks whether the price can't be knocked down a little does. This question exerts less pressure than the statement: 'I want £500 off the price.' An example along the same lines is asking for concessions and indicating a top and bottom limit. Assertions such as: 'The price still has to come down by three or four thousand pounds' or: 'Actually, we have in mind two or three per cent' immediately lead the other party to seize the more favourable figure and then go on negotiating, thus cashing in on the margin.

In such matters, showing a certain resolution is part of the game. A lame attitude of continually putting water in the wine does little for a negotiator's credibility, not only in the eyes of the opponent, but also in the eyes of his constituency. So take care in formulating a 'final proposal'. If you have to yield on your 'final proposal' too often, you make yourself unreliable. On the other hand, too great a fear of loss of face brings negotiations to a deadlock. Concessions are usually inevitable: negotiating is not the same as getting everything you can no matter what the price.

There is another tactic related to concessions that we have not mentioned: allowing things to reach an *impasse*. Allowing an impasse to continue for a while is one way of making it clear that not many more concessions are to be expected. Conversely, impasses can be used to probe the other side's willingness to make concessions and thus to test its determination. Impasses may also help to get new information on the table.

3.4 In conclusion

Negotiating is a process of information exchange that goes on until compromises advantageous to both parties begin to take shape. It is an art to get this process of information exchange going cautiously and step by step, so that the interests and the expectations of both sides gradually come into view. Only when the parties have allowed each other to peer behind their declared positions and arguments do possible solutions begin to take shape.

CHAPTER 4

Influencing the Balance of Power

The course negotiations take is related to the power and dependency relations of the parties involved. Those parties may be unequally interdependent, but negotiating assumes a certain equality between sides. When there are clear power differences, different behaviour occurs: manipulating and exploitative on one side and submissive and compliant on the other. A certain balance of power and an awareness that both parties need each other are necessary conditions for constructive negotiating.

And yet parties do test each other's strengths and probe the precise balance of dependency. The dilemma here is that a stronger position can provide an advantage at the negotiating table, but an opponent does not like to see his own power position weakened and will do everything possible to prevent that happening. If it comes to a clash of strengths, little will emerge from the negotiations, which turn into a power struggle, shifting in the direction of fighting behaviour. So a careful strategy is required: but again, not too careful, because an opponent may regard too little concern for one's own defence as a way to obtain the advantage; it invites him to exploit the situation, as it were. This dilemma is summarized and clarified with examples of tactics in figure 4.1.

Although seeking fundamental changes in the balance of power will generally spark off a fighting situation, there is still a certain margin for shifts at the negotiating table. Participants are always tempted to try to influence this very important factor: if you manage

Figure 4.1 The 'bending versus domineering' dilemma

Bending 1	2	3	4	Domineering 5
Minimal resistance		Preserving a certain balance		Aggressive, trying to dominate
Restrained use of 'favourable facts', pressure is avoided		Attempting to influence the balance by means of facts and restrained pressure		Influencing the balance by means of threats, manipulations, confusion and arrogance
Little resistance when challenged		When challenged, reacts in proportion		When challenged, attacks
No active interest in alternatives to the current relationship		Alert to alternatives for improving one's position *within the current relationship*		Pretending to have a great many alternatives to the current relationship which will be used at the least sign of trouble

to make your opponent more dependent or yourself more independent, it can yield immediate advantage. There are various ways of strengthening one's own power position at the negotiating table, and these are summed up, and their effects discussed, below.

4.1 Tactics for strengthening one's own power position

4.1.1 FIGHTING

These are tactics which are directly aimed at subjugating the opponent, for example:

- ignoring the other party's information and arguments;
- feigning emotions such as anger and impatience;
- not listening, or only listening to 'weak points';
- stating an absolute preference for one's own solution;

- leaving the other party no choice;
- sowing dissension among the other party.

These tactics generally lead to escalation: the other party will soon start to fight back. It is best to use them in small doses if at all. They should not be used as a manner of achieving dominance, but more as a means of obtaining information about how staunchly the other side will uphold its views. One might use them to show a little healthy resistance to fighting behaviour by the other side. The idea is that the pressure should be temporary and not such as gradually to set in motion a process of growing hostility on both sides. A short, direct and hard confrontation is preferable to a series of skirmishes.

4.1.2 MANIPULATING

It is sometimes possible to build up authority in the negotiations by using certain manipulations. This is a delicate strategy, and very dependent on the individual negotiator. It applies a special kind of pressure – special because it aims at a person's norms and values, his relationship with his constituency, his personal characteristics such as intelligence and integrity, and the way in which he conducts himself at the negotiating table.

The risks of this strategy are not small. Indeed, to succeed one must manipulate in the true sense of the word, or subjugate the other without his realizing it. This may be possible with a naïve opponent, but even then there is a strong chance that undirected resentment will build up in the other, which will obstruct future negotiations. The reason I treat it here at all is that it is often tried, despite the risks involved. It can be so casual and covert that the 'victim' cannot discover the reason for the impotence or the resentment and irritation he feels. A quick recognition of exactly what is happening can help a person to respond and thus put the negotiations on a sounder basis. Table 4.1 gives six examples of emotional manipulations, their intended effects on the opponent, and ways of defending oneself against them. These emotional manipulations are meant to be disparaging for the opponent; even more subtle and more difficult to counter are the manipulations that appeal to so-called social conventions (table 4.2). If the latter are performed with enough conviction, an opponent can hardly dodge them. Quite involuntarily, he feels guilty, ashamed and even inferior. He grows uncertain. He hesitates

Table 4.1 Disparaging manipulations

Manipulative behaviour	Intended effect on opponent	Response
Pointing out to the opponent possible criticism by his constituency or public opinion	To arouse a feeling of being threatened, uncertainty	Show indignation, amazement that the other would stoop to such tactics
Demonstrating indomitability and invincible self-confidence	To force the other into a role in which he must ask a favour, because he sees that his use of power has no effect	Be sceptical of the position of the other, gradually show more self-confidence
Stating in so many words that the opponent's reasoning does not hold water	To arouse a feeling of powerlessness because the implication is that other arguments will also be punctured	Politely state that the other did not understand clearly
Asking a rhetorical question about the opponent's behaviour or reasoning	To arouse the tendency to answer the question in the hoped-for way or not to answer and thus feel powerless	Do not answer, but simply say that the other has stated the problem incorrectly
Being 'nice and mean', alternately being friendly and indignant	To arouse uncertainty, to disorientate and intimidate the other	Show a tepid reaction to both friendly and indignant behaviour
Playing 'bluff poker', pretending that one's independence is greater than it actually is	By a show of self-confidence, to make the other unsure of himself, so that he cannot hold his ground	Continue to ask critical questions, react with demonstrative tepidity

and starts to make mistakes. Such manipulations are actually 'fighting techniques'. By using them, a negotiator strikes out at his opponent, with the temporary advantage of strengthening his own position in the talks. This ultimately increases the chance of escalation, because the effect on the other is irritation at his own powerless position.

Table 4.2 Manipulations based on 'decency' and 'fairness'

Manipulative behaviour	Intended effect on opponent	Response
'Being friendly', showing appreciation of opponent	To evoke, according to the rules of etiquette, a friendly (and thus deferential) reaction	Either be friendly (*not* deferential) or ignore it
'Pathetic' requests for the understanding of one's own position	Inclination to grant 'generous' and disinterested favour	Rejection of responsibility
Semblance of incompetence to understand 'complicated' position of opponent	An awareness of a need to explain things, thereby disclosing too much information	Specific questions on what is not understood
Business-like orientation, treating problems as incidental questions	A feeling of 'old boys' who should not make it difficult for each other	Indicate firmly that there are still some obstacles
'Rational–serious' attitude: statement of authority based on 'evidence' and 'constructive' ideas	Fear of seeming stupid, not serious or unconstructive	Assert that some important aspects have not yet been taken into account

4.1.3 FACTS AND EXPERTISE

Expert knowledge, background information, having facts and materials at hand: all of these may strengthen one's position. The manner in which one tries to alter power relations is important. A triumphant attitude, for example, can cause much ill feeling and may put the future relationship under serious pressure.

Sometimes there are 'new facts' which have to do directly with power relations. Examples of 'new facts' are the formation of a stronger coalition or the appearance of *alternatives* to the present dependency relations. The availability of alternatives carries a lot of weight.

Within any organization, policy changes have consequences for the balances of power among the various units. Examples are: emphasizing a particular personnel and organizational policy, giving primacy to technological innovation, giving priority to commercial aspects. The changing balances of power which result from such developments will sooner or later have their effects in a different allocation of scarce resources such as personnel, budgets, investments, space in buildings and other facilities.

4.1.4 EXPLORING

This technique, which we will treat more extensively in chapter 6, can strengthen one's position in several ways. Exploring means taking the initiative: asking questions, presenting information, making proposals, creating a possible package deal. By taking more of these initiatives, one increases one's own strategic leeway. Exploring also implies taking account of the interests of the opponent, the attitude being: 'How do we find a solution to this *together*?' This legitimates a person's performance and lends him authority.

4.1.5 STRENGTHENING THE RELATIONSHIP

The relationship with the opponent can be strengthened by developing acceptance and trust (as described in chapter 5). Other means to this end are developing a stronger common interest and increasing the common ground. To do this means devising and carrying out solutions of interest to both parties in a larger number of areas. These techniques increase mutual dependence: one side cannot use them unilaterally to strengthen its own position. At best, for the one in the less powerful position, a substantial increase of mutual dependency makes the relationship somewhat more symmetrical.

4.1.6 POWER OF PERSUASION

Elements of effective persuasion are:

- a clear, well-structured manner of explaining one's own opinion;
- a reasonably relaxed, but not nonchalant, attitude;
- variation in voice level, tempo, concrete examples and general lines of argument; use of visual aids;
- a deliberate commitment to one's own view, as long as it does not become mere rhetoric.

Manipulating and fighting can provide a temporary advantage, but contain the risk of escalation and irritated personal relations. The other ways are more constructive.

4.2 Strengthening the starting position

Once seated at the negotiating table, opportunities to influence the balance of power are scarce. A negotiator must have consolidated his position before this point is reached. Important sources of power here are:

- Specialized knowledge in certain fields; preferably knowledge that is scarce and of vital importance.
- Having a broad background. Do your homework, have a good overview of the situation, knowledge of what went before, knowledge of policy changes; have all important documents available.
- Having alternatives: not only alternative solutions for the items on the agenda, but also different ways of reaching your own goals, perhaps with others.
- 'Political' access and political intuition. Easy access to relevant centres of power is of crucial importance.
- Status, which may be in terms of tangible success, informal authority, hierarchical position, personal trustworthiness, credibility – all contribute to it.
- Support of others: having allies during the meeting, being able to obtain help and support from other groups not present; not operating in isolation.

These are facts that will show their effectiveness at the negotiating table.

It is also possible to strengthen one's starting position at the negotiating table beforehand in a more manipulative manner. Interesting in this connection are Korda's (1975) directions on how to gain the upper hand unobtrusively from the outset. His instructions for office furnishings, complete with lay-outs, are most entertaining: how to locate the furniture so that the space for the visitor is limited; chairs in which the visitor sinks so deep that he must peform a series of acrobatics to get to the ashtray, which is naturally inaccessible from the chair. Korda often worked out his ideas in their most ludicrous consequences. He described offices that were only accessible along such a route that even the most hardened business-man had become as meek as a mouse before knocking on the door. The door of the office was often solid and bare, without a knob or even a keyhole. Only a buzzer on the desk of the owner or his secre-tary could open it. A female top manager in the publishing world has her office crammed with breakable things, rickety tables, flimsy chairs, etc. A visitor can hardly find room for his briefcase and papers. Other top managers quickly feel like the proverbial bull in a china shop there. Their determination ebbs away, and they become 'spineless', according to the owner of all this apparatus.

Korda's typical proofs of power are amusing in their familiarity.

- Powerful people never get wet or dirty. Even if it is pouring and everyone else comes in soaked, looking dishevelled, powerful people turn up impeccable as if by magic. Moreover, they radiate health and vitality. And they are never troubled by perspiration.
- Powerful people never wait, they let others wait. As if by nature, they are always surrounded by convenience and comfort; for a lunch appointment, for example, even in a packed restaurant, an excellent table is immediately available for them.
- Powerful people never dial telephone numbers, they never make photocopies or even add up figures, they don't type or sharpen pencils. The first sign of power is often a creeping helplessness – people who have been photocopying for years not only no longer want to, but even pretend that they cannot.
- Powerful people often come and go unexpectedly. They enter calmly and resolutely. They take care of their affairs and suddenly they are gone. Somehow or other, doorkeepers, receptionists and secretaries have no hold over them. No one stops them; they stride in unannounced wherever they want.

Do such tactics really work? I am not sure. Korda is undoubtedly exaggerating, but he is a keen observer of the power charge of simple everyday actions and appearances. However, this strong point is also Korda's limitation. He presents a one-sided picture of power, as something that can be reduced to knacks, symbols and rituals.

4.3 Conclusion

All activities at the negotiating table are embedded in the nature of the mutual dependency – how strong, how one-sided, how permanent it is. Negotiations will only take place if there is a certain amount of interdependence: if the balance tips too much to one side, we see entirely different behavioural tendencies: 'requesting', ordering and exploiting versus more submissive and passive or aggressive. Awareness of the continuity of the relationship tempers the impulses towards fighting behaviour.

All activities between parties are coloured and modelled by the balance of power. No wonder negotiators are very sensitive to changes in the power and dependency balances. During a few negotiating sessions, an experiment of mine to trace and analyse the moments of clearly increasing tension in individual negotiators always brought to light changes in the balance of power. Sometimes open challenges were involved, but the case was more often one of covert attempts to alter the balance of power. Both becoming less powerful and becoming more powerful trigger off strong emotional impulses. It can be important to develop one's 'radar' in this field.

Sometimes the causes of a great many tensions at the negotiating table are very difficult to trace, and we tend to attribute them to coincidence or to purely personal phenomena. The following questions can help to trace the roots.

- Is my position in terms of power or influence now at stake in one way or another?
- Am I now strengthening my position, or others theirs?
- What is happening now with the prevailing balance of power among the people involved?
- Am I perhaps being manipulated or more openly driven into a corner?
- Am I, without being aware of it, manipulating or being more openly intimidating?

How negotiating processes are influenced by distinct power differences will be dealt with in detail in chapter 11.

CHAPTER 5

Promoting a Constructive Climate

Good negotiators consider it important to promote a constructive climate and respectful personal relationships. An irritated or very formal atmosphere hampers effective negotiating. So they try to develop trust, acceptance and credibility. In this way they express their interdependence. Examples of tactics in this area are:

- paying attention to each other's opinions;
- promoting informal and open contacts;
- avoiding loss of face;
- behaving predictably and seriously, not using ploys and stratagems or 'pulling a fast one';
- distinguishing role behaviour (e.g. a firm demand) from personal goodwill and mutual respect.

The dilemma a negotiator must face here is that trusting the other without reservation means running the risk of seriously weakening his own position and of overcompromising. What is needed is a kind of calculated trust, compatible with remaining fully aware of the exploitative possibilities of a very personal and confidential relationship. Trust and credibility are important. But at the same time, investing heavily in trust and personal relations may easily be seen either as overbearing, or as weak and inept. Figure 5.1 summarizes the possibilities: one should aim for the area in the middle.If one can combine this with a tenacious stance on substance, one has resolved a classic negotiating problem: how to promote one's own interests

Figure 5.1 The 'jovial versus hostile' dilemma

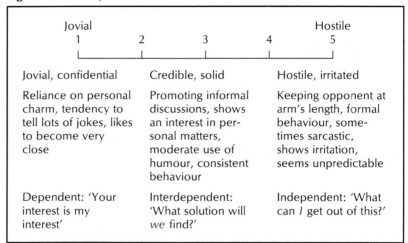

without starting power games or causing personal relations to deteriorate.

We can classify the tactics for coping with this dilemma into three categories:

1 Separating the negotiator as a person from his behaviour that is causing tensions;
2 Avoiding behaviour which causes unnecessary tensions;
3 Using opportunities to reduce tension.

5.1 Separating person and behaviour

In the first place, a clear awareness is needed of everyone's tendency to play the man rather than the ball, particularly when the man shows firm resistance. The temptation to eliminate tension in this way is great. A way to avoid this is to regard a tough attitude on the part of the opponent as typical role behaviour which a person in that position must inevitably exhibit. Put more simply: play the ball, not the man.

If you find you must take a hard stance yourself, there are several ways to help your opponent separate personal relations from negotiating behaviour:

- refer to the constituency;
- appeal to the circumstances;
- state explicitly that your comments are not personally intended;
- put 'incidents' from the past in their proper perspective;
- state in advance that what you are about to say may come across hard.

Experienced negotiators have little difficulty making this separation. On the contrary, they show clear respect for a tenacious attitude (naturally, one supported by facts and arguments). It is very important to develop credibility and acceptance as a person in this context. One way of achieving this is by acquiring more knowledge and understanding of each other. This might take place in informal conversations about more personal matters or about current news. It is important to show some openness about yourself, to show a certain interest in others. Maintaining credibility sometimes demands great care; and integrity, consistency and predictability are important elements in a good personal manner. A negotiator who betrays the confidence in him, for example, by being caught lying, cannot get back on the right side. He has lost his credibility at a single blow. Credibility and trust are so important that there is something to be said for defining negotiating as gradually building up and consolidating sufficient trust to make an agreement possible.

5.2 Avoiding unnecessary tension

A good example of generating unnecessary irritation is emphasizing the term 'reasonable' in talking about one's own party or proposals. Such messages, that we are reasonable, constructive, open, frank, generous, positive, etc., have little persuasive power, but they do carry the implicit connotation that the opponent might very well be unreasonable and unconstructive. Their over-use should therefore be avoided.

The use of questions is also important in this context. Questions can have a positive effect because they show you take an interest. A question can be an acceptable alternative to a flat rejection.

There are more ways in which you can show tact. If you must reject a proposal from your opponent, it is better to state that you *cannot* agree to it rather than that you *will not* agree to it. 'We will not' contains an element of arbitrary choice that 'we cannot' does not have.

Threats can also cause much unnecessary irritation and resistance. It is better to mention the consequences as factually as possible: 'Don't threaten with thunder and lightning, just predict the weather.'

It can also be helpful to announce beforehand what you are about to do at the negotiating table:

'I would like to ask another question . . .'
'I have a suggestion here . . .'
'Something is on my mind . . .'

In general, anything that contributes to an orderly and predictable course of affairs can help to avoid unnecessary tension. I repeat 'unnecessary', because certain tensions are inherent in negotiations and some tension-producing behaviour cannot be avoided. Examples are: impasses, sounding one another out, clearly stating where matters stand and, in more general terms, dealing with dilemmas on the cooperation–fighting continuum. A point which negotiators should keep in mind in this context is causing a loss of face. Catching the opponent off guard, pulling a fast one, letting it be known quite subtly that you know exactly what the other party is after, making the most of the opponent's 'mistakes', are all examples of behaviour that can easily damage the negotiating climate.

Finally, a brief remark about non-verbal behaviour. How do you sit? A slightly relaxed but alert attitude is the best. Try to emanate something of a 'we-feeling', in the sense of 'how can we find a solution together?' Sometimes a negotiator tends to take an exaggeratedly self-confident and independent attitude. Small incidents can then easily provoke reactions of testiness, impatience, hurt or irritation, with a resulting rapid deterioration in the climate.

5.3 Reducing the tension

In addition to a careful choice of words, every negotiating situation offers certain opportunities which, if used, can contribute to a positive atmosphere. For example:

- if any appreciation of the other party is possible, show it;
- try to take account of personal needs;

- listen to the other, respond to his remarks; show respect for his reasoning, even if you do not agree with it;
- show a sense of humour, be able to put your own behaviour into perspective;
- talk informally when appropriate about more personal matters or about current news;
- refer to your mutual dependence; show that you have common interests.

Very important in this connection are the moments just before the negotiations. Everyone is somewhat tense, especially if they expect the meeting to be difficult. A few tips:

- do not take your seat immediately, but put your briefcase where you want to sit and walk around;
- seek informal contact, preferably on a somewhat personal level; talk of outside interests, vacation plans, previous common experiences;
- keep moving, try to greet several of those present and to speak to them;
- be conscious of your posture while standing and when you sit down: avoid being unnecessarily tense and stiff;
- avoid standing in large groups; in a group of five or more people, it is extremely annoying if two hold a conversation while the rest listen on the sidelines.

A good motto for the beginning of negotiations is: share experiences, build up a positive climate.

Once the actual negotiations have started, I find the following two points are important.

1 Show an interest. Try to find out 'the story behind the story'. Ask questions. Show that you have listened by remarks such as: 'If I understand you correctly, you mean . . .' 'Your ideas primarily focus on . . .' 'The most important points in your proposal are . . .' Remember that this has nothing to do with being 'nice'. It is in your interest to know and to understand where your opponents stand.

2 Keep in touch with the undercurrent of feelings. Be attentive to emotional signals in yourself and in others. How tense are you? What sorts of signals are others sending: annoyance, fear, anger, confidence, confusion? Where do these feelings come from? Sometimes emotions can be made the topic of discussion. The key word here is

'dosage'; outbursts should be avoided. It is sometimes possible to speak very matter-of-factly about troublesome emotions and thus to eliminate them: 'Before we go any further, I want to get something off my chest. I was a bit annoyed by . . .; do you feel the same way?' Or: 'We on this side feel we are under extraordinary pressure; whether it is rational or not, our reaction tends toward mistrust and animosity. I think we should do something about this.'

Even without reaching solutions, simply talking can have a liberating effect and prevent escalation. Dealing with real emotions must be distinguished from feigning emotions, which can be used to exert pressure – showing impatience, looking out of the window, slamming your briefcase shut. Feigned emotions can have some effect if used sparingly.

CHAPTER 6

Obtaining Procedural Flexibility

In chapter 3, on obtaining substantial results, several tactics relating to information exchange, choice of position and making concessions were discussed. In addition to a factual choice of position, many of these tactics also imply a strategic choice: trying to give up nothing for as long as possible and to keep open as many options as possible. In this chapter I want to go more systematically into *procedures* which facilitate the exploration of negotiating leeway. However hard and unyielding a position may be, it can still often be combined with great procedural flexibility in seeking favourable compromises. There is more than one way of getting things done! We must distinguish the *means* from the *ends*: some negotiators are well able to combine flexibility of means with sticking to their own goals.

Another fundamental dimension of negotiating behaviour is involved here, a dimension which is at right angles to the cooperating–fighting axis which we have discussed at length. We are talking about the exploring–avoiding axis. The question here is: how explorative is a negotiator? Both practitioners and researchers emphasize the central importance of an actively exploring attitude. Successful negotiators go on energetically seeking alternatives that are relatively satisfactory for both parties, without having to moderate their own demands. This is greatly facilitated by an intensive exchange of information, trying out possible solutions, making tentative proposals, thinking out loud, informally sounding out the other party. The *integrative potential* of the situation is thus fully utilized. Exploring is a search for overlapping interests: are there common premises, are relatively small concessions possible that mean a great deal to the opponent and vice versa, can a combination of mutual advantages be created in a package deal? The two poles of this range of behaviour are shown in figure 6.1.

Figure 6.1 Procedural flexibility: exploring versus avoiding

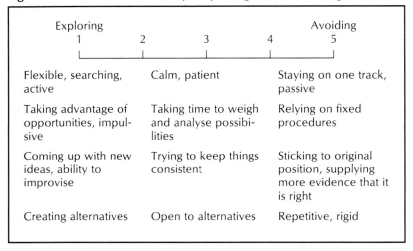

To understand this polarity, it is important to see that a person can be passive in an ostensibly active manner. Examples would be using the same arguments but formulating them differently, clinging tenaciously to original premises, ignoring new information, defending a particular solution through thick and thin, or turning it into a matter of principle. Such behaviour may sometimes be tactically warranted, as long as you are aware that it is a rigid 'more of the same' and puts a stop, at least temporarily, to the search for integrative potential. Even though it looks very active and may be accompanied by much bravado, it is in fact an entrenchment, and can very easily begin to resemble fighting behaviour. We also encounter a more innocent variant of it, in which a person calmly, almost abstrusely, relates his own standpoint and more or less leaves it at that. This keeps matters vague, no-one commits himself, and sometimes people even seem to be in complete agreement. Or, by putting things off, matters are left to take their own course; meanwhile, a person goes his own way, thus avoiding confrontation.

6.1 When to explore

Negotiations go through several *phases*. Depending on the phase, there are several opportunities for exploration. Tough negotiating can be characterized by a sequence of four phases:

1 preparation;
2 verbal fireworks;
3 psychological warfare;
4 crisis and finalization.

These phases occur in negotiations in which substantial interests are at stake and problems with the constituency are a constant threat. This demands great skill and willingness to explore. Many negotiations take a milder course, and the phases can be described in more neutral terms, such as

1 preparation;
2 initial choice of position;
3 search phase;
4 impasse and finalization.

Exploration is easier in these situations. The point is that hard negotiating, despite all the problems it can cause, can be very well combined with exploring. It should be emphasized that exploring has nothing to do with being 'soft', amicable or yielding. What it is about is well expressed in the following rule of thumb: be *firm* but *flexible*.

Each phase in the negotiating process offers opportunities to explore. We will see that a model of different phases can be used as a procedural technique to increase flexibility. The most important procedures will be worked out in the form of tactics in the second part of this chapter, 'tactics for exploring'.

6.1.1 THE PREPARATORY PHASE

Experienced negotiators always emphasize the importance of this phase, in which people determine not only their interests and positions, but also their strategy. At the furthest extreme this comprises a scenario of steps to be taken and responses to all the alternatives you can possibly think of. Such a scenario can be tried out and adapted among yourselves by holding 'trial' negotiations. A thorough preparation generally means a tendency for positions to harden, thus diminishing the chances of an agreement. This can be overcome by exploring in two ways: in informal consultation, or by setting down alternatives.

In informal consultation, the parties work toward an exchange of ideas on standpoints, common interests and background situations. They probe reactions, sound out what might be attainable. Decisions are not made. The parties avoid taking inviolable positions. No report is made. The parties are getting a feeling for how much room there is to manoeuvre, while their priorities are taking shape. Informal consultation might take place in a joint study group, an agenda committee or preliminary meetings.

If we can manage to concentrate on alternatives during the preparatory phase, we prevent people from sitting down at the negotiating table with more or less immutable positions. Brainstorming may be very helpful at this point: do not invest effort in the best standpoint, but in interesting options. The more alternatives, the better. One should avoid starting out on negotiations from an internal compromise obtained with great difficulty. An internal compromise is sometimes quickly outmoded, resulting in frustration and wasted energy.

6.1.2 INITIAL CHOICE OF POSITION

The beginning of the actual negotiations sometimes starts before the parties sit down at the table. Parties present statements which contain an initial choice of position. There is a tendency to present one's own position as final and entirely logical, often in the form of assertive statements. People present their proposals, well supported by facts and arguments, as fair and reasonable. There is sometimes a tendency to make open or covert criticism of others. Faced with this, outsiders often fear the worst. How can a compromise ever be reached? More experienced negotiators will shrug their shoulders. This phase serves two purposes: to show the constituency that you have their interests at heart, and to define the playing field while trying to reserve as much space as possible on it for yourself. The exploratory side of this phase could consist of being attentive to signals from the various parties about where the primary issues and interests lie.

The more a person concentrates his initial choice of position on his view of the situation – the interests behind it, bottlenecks he wants to eliminate, objectives, assumptions – and the less on his specific standpoint in the form of particular demands, the better this works. The former creates leeway and more opportunities to see points in common. In the latter case, a deadlock of claim against claim, position versus position, proposal and counterproposal will more readily arise, and the negotiation more quickly turns into barter without looking into the chances of integration. People must allow each other this opportunity to clarify their own views, and must not give in to the temptation to 'set matters straight', for this will only lead to time-consuming arguing. Exploring here means asking questions to investigate and define the interests and the assumptions behind them.

6.1.3 SEARCH PHASE

Discussions follow in which both sides try to find out how earnestly the other side will defend its demands. People continue to present their own choice of position as a logical answer which is in the common interest. They look for flexibility, for openings. Broadly speaking, there are two ways of exploring in this phase. Their forms, however, are almost diametrically opposed.

Exploring by means of pressure
Bluffing, threatening, increasing time pressure, refuting the arguments of the other party, brandishing the common interest are examples of pressure tactics. It may look hard and fierce. There is a risk of escalation. And yet a great deal of information can be gathered during this phase. Reactions from the other side give indications of what is attainable. And the other side is entitled to know your priorities. So a little extra pressure for concessions by the other side on their top priorities can be a warranted means of obtaining information.

Exploring by means of a 'non-binding search'
Asking questions, trying out ideas, thinking out loud, once again going over the consequences of a particular idea, working out a point 'for fun', formulating a tentative proposal, formulating 'unripe' ideas for a solution, brainstorming: these are all ways of probing the integrative leeway.

Sometimes the two ways are alternated. In this way, the parties test each other while sounding out the possibilities for combinations of wishes and interests. The negotiations can sometimes even take on the nature of a joint search in which all kinds of ideas and alternatives are actively combined and probed, preferably with no obligation. Purposely created misunderstandings throw matters into confusion. On the face of it, everything is still shrouded in mist. Nothing important is finished, everything still seems open. Yet gradually the contours of a possible agreement become clear. The reactions of their constituencies give the negotiators some idea as to how far they can go.

So much happens during this phase that we can sometimes speak of three subphases: first, vigorous *detailed deliberations* in which both sides may use strong pressure; then a *maturation phase*; finally a *phase of cooperative seeking*. These subphases may repeat themselves.

6.1.4 IMPASSE AND FINALIZATION

Pressure and confusion may lead up to a crisis-like atmosphere. At a certain point – sometimes under the pressure of a time limit – it becomes clear that matters are not getting any further. Often the constituency must be consulted. An impasse may be needed to cause a compromise to crystallize. It is necessary as the final test of how strong the various interests and positions are. An impasse may appear in various forms: the matter has been deadlocked for some time. Various proposals are on the table, but no agreement has been reached. A repetition of positions goes on and on.

It may be very hard for inexperienced negotiators to restrain themselves from fighting behaviour at this point. More experienced negotiators have less difficulty with it, although this does not guarantee that things will turn out well. Impasses have two exploratory possibilities: they provide information about how rigorous the standpoints are, and they can give an impetus to creativity. Impasses are a sort of test of how tenacious parties are; they force people to look for leeway once more. At the same time they impel people towards a search for new, more creative solutions. This demands a business-like attitude. One cannot give in to the tendency to hardening and escalation, but must continue to search.

These phases can crystallize into unwritten but very strict *rules*: negotiating becomes a sort of ritual. Some diplomatic talks are a good example of this. A ritualized form of negotiating tends to reduce tensions and uncertainties. Its course becomes fairly predictable. It greatly increases opportunities to control and regulate conflicts. A disadvantage is that such a process may take a good deal of time.

6.2 Tactics for exploring

We will now elaborate the various tactics used in exploring. All negotiating partners have their own responsibility in this. By making the proper procedural proposals, a chairman can naturally facilitate exploring. How he can best do this is explained in chapter 10, 'Chairing Negotiations'.

6.2.1 INFORMAL ADVANCE CONSULTATION

Parties try to exchange ideas about each other's standpoints and background situations. Actual negotiation is taboo. Decisions are not made. Hard standpoints are not taken. No report is made.

6.2.2 ALWAYS BEGIN THE NEGOTIATIONS WITH AN EXPLORATORY PHASE

Particularly when there are already proposals on the table, this is easier said than done. There is a strong tendency to react to one another's proposals. Do not confuse argumentation with exploration! In debating, people defend their own proposals and try to weaken those of the other party. In the long run, so much energy is invested in their own detailed standpoints that the margins become almost nil. They cannot even consider anything else without a serious loss of face.

6.2.3 ASK QUESTIONS

What do people want to achieve? What is the objective behind it? What possibilities have been considered? How did they arrive at their proposals?

6.2.4 SHOW A GOOD EXAMPLE

Give information about goals, about other possibilities that have been discussed, about what you ultimately hope to achieve in this way, what your basic assumptions are.

6.2.5 TRY TO FIND COMMON CRITERIA

Do the basic assumptions show any common ground? Are there norms and values that appeal to both parties? Are there policy statements which commit the parties?

There is a risk inherent in this: parties may start negotiating at length about assumptions and principles. Parties sometimes hope to gain concrete advantages by elevating certain statements to the level of principles. If care is not taken, the result may be very lengthy negotiations about high-flown ideals. For parties will refuse to endorse criteria and principles unfavourable to them unless they are formulated in such complex or abstract terms that they can be interpreted to their advantage in the 'real' negotiations. In that case, a hard round of negotiations will have been completed, the value of which is slight. This is a serious risk, as parties are often superbly capable of linking their wants to higher principles. This can give rise to bombastic prose that has nothing to do with negotiating. If no clear, workable criteria can be found, there are three other tangible options:

- focusing on common interests;
- having parties present alternative proposals;
- working with a 'platform proposal'.

These options are covered below.

6.2.6 TRY TO FIND COMMON INTERESTS

Parties are interdependent, they need each other. What binds them is the overlap in interests. What will benefit both parties? Is there anything common to their interests? Be clear about your interests. Concrete details, specific information, consequences, etc., bring your interests to life; they help legitimate them, in the eyes of your opponent as well. Even if you do not agree with them, try to view the interests of the other side at least as *part of the problem*. Listen closely, repeat them if necessary in your own words. By asking questions, check whether you have understood them correctly.

6.2.7 TRY TO GET AS MANY ALTERNATIVES ON THE TABLE AS POSSIBLE

- Do not commit yourself to a solution in the preparatory phase. Discuss in what direction a solution should be sought. Discuss possible solutions. Create room to manoeuvre.
- Try to have informal or 'preliminary deliberations' with the other parties. Probe each other's ideas and avoid choosing a pronounced position. At most, try to line up a few alternatives without anyone having to commit himself.
- Informal contacts during the negotiations can be used to drum up possible alternatives.
- Try to get as many alternatives as possible on the table in the negotiations themselves. Hold a stocktaking/brainstorming phase. Suggestions are welcome; do not pass judgement on them or argue against them too quickly.
- Increase the negotiating leeway. Discussing several topics over a longer period of time may increase the chance of a package deal which is relatively favourable to both parties.
- Use the expertise of professionals and other disciplines.
- Divide the negotiating leeway over different sorts of issues. If an all-embracing solution is not possible, it still leaves open the possibility of a partial one. If agreement cannot be reached on the substance, then perhaps it can on the procedure. A tentative agreement may not be as good as a definitive one, but it is something. Even though they may be but a tiny fraction of the whole, there are always issues for which solutions can be found. An agreement 'without obligation' is a small gain compared to a binding one, but it is often better than nothing.

6.2.8 MAKE A 'PLATFORM PROPOSAL'

A procedural step which can work very well is making a proposal and then amending it with other parties. Instead of defending your own proposal through thick and thin, you simply ask under what conditions it would be acceptable to the other, what alterations the other party would like. It also gives you an opportunity to make suggestions of your own. A proposal can be amended in this way until an acceptable compromise has been reached. This method can work very well, especially if the issues are complex and several parties are involved. A broad proposal is made. This outline is filled in and elaborated in several rounds of talks.

6.2.9 ALLOW EACH OTHER TO SCORE

An important integrative potential often lies here. The more agenda items and issues, the greater is the chance of interesting combinations. It would be quite a coincidence if the issues that are of primary importance to one party were to have precisely the same priority for the other party. A relatively modest concession by one party sometimes means considerable profit for the other. Try to find these points: what can the other gain which will cost you little? Knowledge of the priorities of the constituencies can be of help here.

6.2.10 PROGRESS BY MEANS OF NEW PROPOSALS

If an impasse continues, a new proposal may be a good tactic. Alternatives developed at an earlier stage can prove their usefulness here. A good technique is sometimes to incorporate the least objectionable elements of the last proposal of the opponents in your own proposal.

6.2.11 PROGRESS BY MEANS OF A STUDY GROUP

Sometimes it is possible to end threatened impasses and fruitless debates by creating a study group. Parties meet in a somewhat different composition to set down alternatives and to develop an initiative for a possible compromise. No report is made, no-one writes anything down. An agenda committee can be used for the same purpose.

6.2.12 EXPLORING DURING IMPASSES

Impasses can freeze personal relations as well as positions. To keep matters moving, the following tactics may be used. Note that none of these tactics is a concession. They involve behaviour that promotes change rather than behaviour with a cooling and rigidifying effect.

- look for more and different information instead of correcting information and assessing it negatively;
- look for the problems that lie at the root of the impasse instead of convincing and threatening;
- be more spontaneous rather than more formal; more creative rather than more repetitive;
- emphasize equality and mutual dependency (for instance, by exploring the negative consequences of a lasting impasse) rather than acting superior or withdrawing;
- show your disillusionment instead of acting as if it does not matter;
- adjourn and seek informal contact rather than sitting out the meeting.

If you find that your attempts to explore get no response and if you want to apply some pressure, 'cultivating an impasse' is sometimes a good tactic. Be approachable but undertake little: silence, long pauses, strolling around, looking out of the window, drinking coffee, cleaning your pipe, talking with colleagues about other matters are ways of doing this.

In summary, the tactics discussed in this chapter can be combined into three strategic groups.

1 *Treat several issues simultaneously*. Do not deal with them one by one, but 'juggle' several issues at the same time in search of an optimal package deal. Go through the agenda *in breadth* rather than digging *in depth* on points where it is not easy to reach agreement. A simple procedural technique to facilitate this is the stipulation that nothing will be finalized until everything has been worked through.

2 *Furnish an agreement from the 'helicopter' point of view*. This means working towards solutions and compromises after reaching a diagnosis that is as complete as possible of the interests and mutual dependencies behind them. Scanning possible options and alternatives is also a part of this. Often, an effective procedural step is to make a broad platform proposal and use it as an outline for further amendment and elaboration until a compromise has been reached.

3 *Creativity*. Brainstorming, thinking out loud, continuing to search for slightly different combinations, formulating inventively, keeping procedural ideas at hand to keep things moving in impasses, being

able to step outside of the initially delineated field. This demands great energy and *power of imagination*. Less enterprising minds will sometimes call this opportunism. They forget that tenaciously held self-interest is usually behind this flexibility.

6.3 Conclusion

We have discussed a very important dimension of negotiating behaviour: the exploring–avoiding dimension which lies at right angles to the 'cooperation–fighting' axis. Exploring has proved to be a way of linking cooperation to competition, interdependence to interests. The rule of thumb 'be firm but flexible' expresses something of this. Starting from mutual but divergent interests, utilize the integrative space. This demands creativity and flexibility, linked with an attitude of 'how do we find a way out together'. A fighting climate is an obstacle to such an attitude. Some negotiators very consciously work on promoting a certain informality and on reducing tensions, not by keeping them in check, but by letting them penetrate to them emotionally and then working through them. It may be helpful to:

- slow down the tempo, adjourn;
- recognize tension in your own attitude (breathing) and briefly 'go along' with it, then consciously relax;
- keep your sense of humour, see matters in perspective;
- express tensions and emotions with measure.

Acting as if indifferent to the outcome or becoming more formal is only counterproductive.

CHAPTER 7

Influencing the Constituency

The relationship with the constituency is important to negotiators. Much of the behaviour at the negotiating table in fact cannot be explained without reference to this dimension. Often there is even a sort of 'gentlemen's agreement' between negotiators on such points as:

- one party does not make a fool of the other in front of his constituency;
- one party allows the other a substantial 'show' now and then;
- one party does not make concessions too quickly, in order not to arouse unrealistic expectations among the constituency of the other party.

The most essential characteristic of the relationship with the constituency is its negotiating nature. Many naïve negotiators are not sufficiently aware of this. We could even go so far as to say that the core of successful negotiating must be sought in wanting to and being able to negotiate with the constituency. The negotiations with the opponents come only in second place. This may sound a little exaggerated, but there are pitfalls and limitations attached to this essentially negotiating relationship. The five most important pitfalls are the following:

1 We do not see it as a negotiating relation, so we good-naturedly go along with what the constituency asks of us.
2 We are incapable of negotiating with the constituency because

there we must deal with persons who are more powerful in a hierarchical or formal sense.

3 We are incapable of negotiating with the constituency because we got into the position of negotiator by making large promises to the constituency.

4 We are incapable of negotiating with the constituency because we allowed ourselves to be pinned down to a precisely-worded mandate in preliminary talks with the constituency.

5 We have allowed ourselves to be provoked by the constituency. This not only applies to the factual stand taken, which is seldom tempered by a constituency but, on the contrary, tends to be radicalized by it. This pitfall also applies to the climate and the balance of power. The constituency can very easily evolve an oversimplified and stereotyped image of the opponent, an image in which the negative aspects begin to gain more and more dominance. This makes it hard to take a realistic view of the opponent. Parallel to this negative image, a tendency often arises to deal firmly with the opponent. This implies escalation to a situation in which the constituency aims to subjugate the opponent. Negotiators may have a difficult time resisting such pressure from the constituency, mainly because, if they go along with it, their own position relative to the constituency is strengthened: their leadership is less disputed and their credibility increases.

The dilemma in these five points is that while it may be very tempting to go along with the constituency for these reasons, to do so actually reduces the chances of obtaining results with the opponent. Figure 7.1 shows this dilemma, with examples of related tactics.

Negotiating in front of the constituency diminishes the chances of an agreement by which one's own party, in view of the mutual dependency, stands to gain. Negotiators who do not feel particularly bound by their constituency generally turn out to obtain the best results for them.

On the other hand, a casual relationship with the constituency means that a negotiator loses his credibility for his opponents: 'On whose behalf is he really here?' 'Does he have enough influence to carry his constituency?' A good relationship with the constituency involves knowing what is on their minds and being seen by them as their representatives, while at the same time having sufficient leeway

Figure 7.1 The 'uncommitted versus overcommitted' dilemma

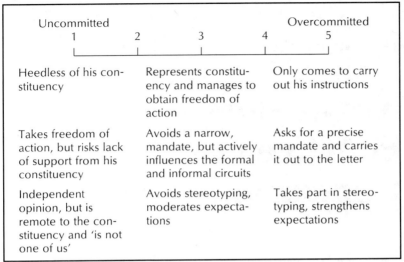

Uncommitted				Overcommitted
1	2	3	4	5
Heedless of his constituency		Represents constituency and manages to obtain freedom of action		Only comes to carry out his instructions
Takes freedom of action, but risks lack of support from his constituency		Avoids a narrow, mandate, but actively influences the formal and informal circuits		Asks for a precise mandate and carries it out to the letter
Independent opinion, but is remote to the constituency and 'is not one of us'		Avoids stereotyping, moderates expectations		Takes part in stereotyping, strengthens expectations

to make compromises which very often fall short of the constituency's demands. Just try that as a negotiator! It often happens that negotiators, in order to ensure success, have to negotiate at least as firmly with their constituency as with their opponents. In fact, everything that is said in this book about negotiating with opponents is in principle applicable to negotiations with the constituency as well.

There are several tactics which are of special help in negotiating with the constituency. The most important are:

- avoid a strict mandate or a precisely formulated task by making the preparatory time short or by keeping the matter confused;
- moderate the demands of the constituency by giving tactical information about what is attainable;
- keep people whose expectations are too high outside the actual negotiations, for instance, by keeping the negotiating team small or by appointing them in subcommittees;
- keep the results of the negotiations vague or more complicated, so that criticism has little basis;
- exaggerate concessions by the opponent.

If this does not help, the negotiator can still employ his personal power and prestige. In the most extreme case, he can resort to putting his own position at stake.

CHAPTER 8

Negotiating Effectively: Conclusions

'Being interdependent while having interests which are in contrast to those of the other party.' This is the problem negotiators must face. To cope with this, I have worked out a model of negotiation. The core of this model consists of two characteristic dimensions of negotiating behaviour.*

1 How does a negotiator cope with the tension between cooperation and fighting? His style of coping is determined by the extent to which his attitude and manner express the interdependency, the relationship, as opposed to a more aggressive and domineering attitude. The two poles of this behaviour are shown in figure 8.1.

2 How explorative is a negotiator? We have already clarified the central importance of an active procedural attitude on the part

---

* These two dimensions are fundamental not only to my model of negotiating, but also to a large number of other investigations and studies on interpersonal behaviour. For example, I mention Horney (1945), who distinguished between 'moving away', 'moving against' and 'moving toward'. Or Schutz (1958), with his fundamental interpersonal orientations: 'inclusion' (behaviour that varies from very intensive involvement to complete distance), 'control' and 'affection'. Schutz also gave a survey of more than twenty authors who arrived at these same fundamental orientations. Zaleznik and Kets de Vries (1975, p. 154) used the same two dimensions in their study on 'managerial power'. They can also be found in familiar behavioural science instruments such as the 'managerial grid' of Blake and Mouton (1969), to chart managerial behaviour, and Thomas's (1979) 'conflict grid' to clarify styles of dealing with conflict.

Figure 8.1 Negotiating behaviour: the 'conceding–stubborn' axis

lenient,   fighting,
jovial,   forceful,
personal   aggressive

     1   2   3   4   5

friendly,   persistent,
open,   calculating
cooperative

of negotiators. We have also seen that, depending on the phase of the negotiations, there are different ways to explore. The two poles of this dimension of negotiating behaviour are shown in figure 8.2.

The conceding–stubborn axis has four aspects. All four of them, each in a different way, are characterized by the tension between cooperation and fighting. In this sense, they are dilemmas. The aspects differ because each of them proceeds from different intentions. All four types of activities are important at the negotiating table. They are shown in table 8.1 together with the dimension of procedural flexibility as a fifth important activity. This dimension also aims at substance, but mainly in a procedural sense. Its intention is to influence the manner of negotiating, the procedures, in such a way that the integrative space can be explored.

This negotiating model is descriptive in the sense that it can be used to describe the behaviour of negotiators. It is also prescriptive

Figure 8.2 Negotiating behaviour: the 'exploring–avoiding' axis

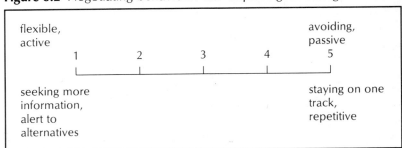

flexible,   avoiding,
active   passive

     1   2   3   4   5

seeking more   staying on one
information,   track,
alert to   repetitive
alternatives

Table 8.1 Summary of negotiating model

Negotiating as five types of activities, each with a different goal	Negotiating as dilemma behaviour	Examples of tactics
I Obtaining substantial results *Goal*: favourable compromise	Conceding v. stubborn 1 2 3 4 5 Lenient, indulgent Tenacious Hard, stubborn	Firm presentation of facts and arguments, creating 'change', blowing up small concessions, working with deadlines, allowing impasses to occur, making a proposal when the time is ripe
II Influencing the balance of power *Goal*: equilibrium or slight domination	Bending v. domineering 1 2 3 4 5 Minimal resistance Preserving a certain balance Aggressive, trying to dominate	Presentation of new facts favourable to yourself, letting it be known you have alternatives, being manipulative, flooring the other party and being coercive now and then, taking and keeping the initiative
III Promoting a constructive climate *Goal*: positive personal relations	Jovial v. hostile 1 2 3 4 5 Confidential, jovial Credible, solid Sarcastic, formal, unpredictable	Promoting informal discussion, humour, showing an interest in matters, being consistent, showing something of the interdependency. Taking care not to cause a loss of face, separating role behaviour from the person
IV Obtaining procedural flexibility *Goal*: flexibility	Exploring v. avoiding 1 2 3 4 5 Flexible, searching, active Calm, patient Staying on one track, repetitive	Searching for new information, enumerating alternative solutions, trying out ideas, adjourning to sound out ideas 'informally', brainstorming, thinking out loud about tentative proposals, calling a study group, working with a platform proposal

Negotiating as five types of activities, each with a different goal	Negotiating as dilemma behaviour	Examples of tactics
V Influencing the constituency	Uncommitted v. overcommitted 1 2 3 4 5 Pays no Represents Merely attention constitu- carries out to con- ency while his instruc- stituency retaining tions leeway	Moderating expectations, preventing stereotyping, keeping hair-splitters out of the delegation, utilizing opportunities for 'drama', keeping the mandate vague, informally influencing opinion leaders
Goal: winning over constituency		

because it can specify what constructive negotiating is all about. In other words, this model helps in the attempt to reach a better knowledge and understanding of negotiating problems. The model also works in therapy and prevention: it shows how we can solve and avoid problems.

So far we have explained the essence of the various activities and dilemmas. We have also tried to increase the reader's 'versatility' in these five fields by discussing a great many different tactics. Below I want to integrate these various strands by discussing constructive and less constructive combinations of activities. We will now work out in more detail and point by point what grip can be derived from this model of negotiating.

8.1 Guidelines

8.1.1 BE FIRM BUT FLEXIBLE

This is a golden rule of experienced negotiators. What does it mean? Link tenacity on your interests to procedural flexibility. (See figure 8.3; in this and the following two diagrams, the arrows indicate the desirable range of behaviour.)

Figure 8.3 Negotiating behaviour: firm but flexible

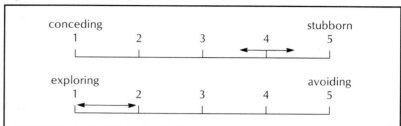

It is quite possible to combine a persistent defence of your own interests with respect for one another and a good climate. (See figure 8.4.)

Figure 8.4 Negotiating behaviour: tenacious but with respect for the other

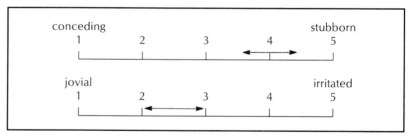

8.1.3 AVOID POWER STRUGGLES

Persistently pursuing your own interests does not necessarily imply a power struggle. Scoring points, being obstinate, threatening, becoming emotional, finding fault, snowing your opponent under with arguments, have little to do with negotiating. (See figure 8.5.)

8.1.4 CULTIVATE A SENSE OF PERSPECTIVE

See the behaviour of the 'opponent' in its proper proportions. For example, some tough and uncompromising statements are primarily aimed at the constituency. In terms of table 8.1, they may look like I,

Figure 8.5 Negotiating behaviour: tenacious, but not a power struggle

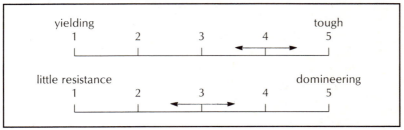

II or III, but they are really V. Recognize moves aimed at the climate for what they are: informal contact. You should not allow yourself to be walked over, but neither should you misuse them by pinning your opponents down to everything they say. Do not react with irritation to a person who offers tough resistance on substance. You might think: 'If only someone else were there.' Another normal reaction is: 'On that chair, with that cap, I wouldn't do any better.'

Negotiating always contains something of a contest, a reciprocal challenge. When challenged, it is usually wise to show some resistance. The chance of reaching a compromise on substance or of creating a constructive atmosphere need not suffer from this. On the contrary, if you do not show some resistance, you merely encourage exploitative behaviour.

Sometimes the behaviour on the power axis is very difficult to perceive. It is disguised as something else, wrapped in another aspect: 'playing the injured party', or 'We can't take that back to our constituency'; or expressing appreciation of the good atmosphere while pushing an issue through; or a person may try to prove he is intrinsically 'right' by appealing to 'excellent reports' and 'top experts'. Recognize such moves as manipulations and do not allow yourself to be confused by them.

8.1.5 REALIZE THAT IMPASSES ARE INEVITABLE

When parties adopt tough stances in the struggle for a result favourable to themselves, impasses and crisis events are inevitable. It's all in the game. Reproaches, tirades, acting injured – all these will perhaps relieve some personal tension and irritation, but they also raise the chances of escalation. In an impasse, do not allow the collision on substance to contaminate the other aspects of negotiating. Ways of dealing with an impasse are to:

- adjourn;
- summarize the various standpoints;
- make a small concession, or offer the prospect of one;
- if the impasse continues, together explore the alternatives and their consequences;
- change the composition of the delegation;
- change the location;
- present an altered proposal;
- postpone the difficult aspect of the negotiations until later;
- call in a third party;
- hold an informal study group: brainstorm about possible solutions;
- take a small part of the problem and reach agreement on this;
- systematically enumerate the solutions once again;
- sound out a key figure of the other delegation during the break.

8.1.6 REMEMBER YOUR CONSTITUENCY

Be aware that the relationship with the constituency is also a negotiating relation. Examples of frequently used tactics are to:

- avoid a strict mandate or a precisely formulated task by keeping the preparation time short or matters confused;
- moderate the demands of the constituency by giving tactical information about what is feasible;
- keep persons whose expectations are too high outside the actual negotiations, for instance, by keeping the negotiating team small or by appointing them in subcommittees;
- keep the results of the negotiations vague or quite complicated, so that criticism has little basis;
- exaggerate concessions by the opponent.

8.1.7 KNOW YOUR OWN STYLE

Develop an awareness of your own style, and develop your own flexibility in the areas which you have not yet really mastered. For instance, are you skilled at the exploring tactics described in chapter 6?

Score yourself on the axes in the figures! Where do you usually operate, to what behaviour do you tend under pressure? Where do you think that your opponents would place you?

8.1.8 REALIZE THAT DOUBTS ARE NORMAL

Be aware that negotiators are permanently on the horns of several dilemmas. Doubt readily crops up, for instance, about whether you were too tough or too lenient, too open or too closed, too friendly or too irritated.

8.2 Limitations

Negotiations presume the existence of a certain amount of leeway, however slight. If there is none, there is nothing to negotiate. Everything is negotiable, provided you get in early enough and at the right level. If that is not possible, then perhaps the 'how' is negotiable!

In addition, negotiating presumes a certain symmetry in the balance of power. The more out of balance the power relations are in the perception of those involved, the less chance there is of negotiating.

8.3 The heart of the model

A summary of the above conclusions yields the following picture. Skilful negotiating revolves first and foremost around a mix of four activities:

1 obtaining substantial results;
2 influencing the balance of power;
3 promoting a constructive climate;
4 obtaining procedural flexibility.

1 *Obtaining substantial results*. This involves a choice of position as expressed in standpoints, proposals, arguments and concessions. Firmly going after your interests and building up a compromise which is as favourable as possible for you are the basic strategies.

2 *Influencing the balance of power*. Attempts to tilt the balance of power are inevitable, and meeting them with little resistance provokes exploitative behaviour. But wanting to dominate, scoring points and being obstinate lead more readily to fighting than to negotiation. Choices can be set out on the bending–domineering axis.

3 *Promoting a constructive climate*. How does one cope with personal relations? This behaviour can be set out on the jovial–hostile axis. Hard negotiating must not be confused with hostile, irritated or sulky behaviour. Being jovial and overbearing does not work either.

4 *Obtaining procedural flexibility*. This is how a negotiator develops integrative potential. How does he create flexibility, how does he maintain other options, how does he find integrative possibilities? This is primarily a question of procedures.

In the activities under 2 and 3, we have seen that it is best to aim at the middle of the range on the axis. Combined with tenacity of substance, they hold the solution to a classic negotiating problem: how to promote one's own interests without being aggressive or hostile. The combination of procedural flexibility with tenacity of substance is also the solution to a second classic negotiating problem: how to promote one's own interests without being obstinate. Or: how to look for solutions jointly without giving in. The solutions to both problems once again underscore the 'both–and' nature of the model described here. It is possible to integrate apparently contradictory types of behaviour.

It all boils down to the fact that one must be able to recognize the various types of negotiating activities and to differentiate them in one's behaviour. It is as simple as that. They tend to 'contaminate' one another in a naïve negotiator. If he takes a tough stance on the content, then he will also tend to act irritated and to sulk, he will want to score points, he will behave rather rigidly and stick to one track. His tough stance will come across as even tougher than strictly necessary. A negotiator who is able to distinguish the dimensions will provoke less resistance and give the impression of being much more reasonable (which he is). And yet he is not a bit more yielding than his 'tough' colleague: he is often even tougher. He concentrates his tenacity on his substantial goal: a tangible compromise which is as advantageous as possible for him. He realizes that an irritated atmosphere does not strengthen but weakens his position. He knows that scoring points or driving the other into a corner have nothing to do with negotiating. He is aware that mutual dependency can benefit *both* parties. He is also aware of the fact that it is in his own interest to influence relations positively for the sake of the continuity of the relationship.

The only other important recommendation has to do with the negotiating phases as a procedural technique to develop flexibility. Briefly summarized: start with a *diagnosis* of mutual premises and interests; investigate where interests overlap and keep an eye on the priorities of both sides. Scanning other options and *alternatives* is also part of this. Then, introducing a very broad '*platform proposal*' is often an effective procedural step: the proposal can serve as an outline for *amendment and alteration* which continue until a compromise is reached. Using these phases can help to prevent the situation from developing into inflexible arguments about positions. We are now in a position to give a profile of effective negotiating. Table 8.2 specifies the tendencies of an effective negotiator. These are behavioural tendencies, not hard-and-fast rules; exceptions are always possible. The diagram also shows a profile of a naïve negotiator.

Finally, it should be remarked that the constituency poses additional problems. It is important to see the relationship with the constituency as a negotiating relation, too.

Figure 8.6 summarizes the most important elements of the model of negotiating described here. The background of all these elements is a degree of *interdependence*. This means that all the elements are influenced by that interdependence. At the negotiating table, people try to alter others' perception of it: these are the activities aimed at altering the balance of power.

8.4 Conclusion

This negotiating model is intended as a means for negotiators to obtain a realistic orientation. It enables negotiators to understand better activities at the negotiating table, their own behaviour included, and to react to it effectively. In essence, it is a view of negotiating as different types of activities.

Table 8.2 Two negotiating profiles

Negotiating as four types of activities, each with a different goal	Most important dilemmas	Examples of tactics
I Obtaining substantial results *Goal*: favourable compromise	Conceding *v.* stubborn 1 2 3 4 5 Lenient, indulgent Tenacious Hard, stubborn	Firm presentation of facts and arguments, creating 'change', blowing up small concessions, working with deadlines, allowing impasses to occur, coming up for your interests and sticking to basic premises
II Influencing the balance of power *Goal*: equilibrium or slight domination	Bending *v.* domineering 1 2 3 4 5 Minimal resistance Preserving a certain balance Aggressive, trying to dominate	Presentation of new facts favourable to yourself, letting it be known you have alternatives to the present relationship, being manipulative, flooring the other party and being coercive now and then, taking and keeping the initiative
III Promoting a constructive climate *Goal*: positive personal relations	Jovial *v.* hostile 1 2 3 4 5 Confidential, jovial Credible, solid Sarcastic, formal, unpredictable	Promoting informal discussion, humour, showing an interest in matters, being consistent, showing something of the interdependence. Taking care not to cause a loss of face, separating role behaviour from the person
IV Obtaining procedural flexibility *Goal*: flexibility	Exploring *v.* avoiding 1 2 3 4 5 Flexible, searching, active Calm, patient Staying on one track, repetitive profile of effective negotiating profile of naïve negotiating	Searching for new information, enumerating alternative solutions, trying out ideas, adjourning to sound out ideas 'informally', brainstorming, thinking out loud about tentative proposals, calling a study group, working with a platform proposal

Figure 8.6 Elements of negotiating model

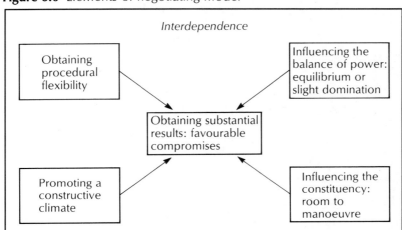

The model can foster the development of an individual's negotiating skill in two ways: by giving him a better mastery of each activity in itself – the tactics mentioned can help in this – and by enabling him to use the activities in varying combinations. Which combinations are most effective has been described above.

The model makes use of distinctions and behavioural rules which are in themselves simple. The reader will have no difficulty in recognizing them, and may even feel that he has brought many of them into practice already. Expressing them in an integrative model may help the reader in further developing his negotiating skill by giving him a more conscious and clearer picture of what it is all about.

PART III

Special Situations and Problems

CHAPTER 9

Preparing Negotiations

In preparing negotiations, the following five areas need attention: the contents, the climate, the balance of power, the constituency and the procedures.

Broadly speaking, three steps can be distinguished in the preparations.

1 Diagnosis: collecting and exchanging information on contents, climate, balance of power and constituency.
2 Goal: identifying the desired result.
3 Procedures: the tactical and strategic preparation. The most important elements are:
   ○ working with alternatives to remain flexible;
   ○ developing a tactical repertory of opening moves;
   ○ formulating a general strategic plan.

There are some indications that experienced and successful negotiators spend their preparation time differently from less experienced and/or less successful negotiators. Experienced negotiators tend to spend more time on the diagnosis and less time on the goals; they spend considerably more time on developing alternatives, and less time on tactical matters. There is, however, little difference between the two in a general strategic sense. Table 9.1 gives an idea of these differences. Perhaps the most striking discrepancy is the difference in the amount of preparation time spent on developing alternatives: successful negotiators spend three times as long on it as the novices.

Table 9.1 Allocation of preparation time by experienced and inexperienced negotiators

Activity	Time spent (%)	
	Inexperienced	Experienced
Diagnosis	16	25
Goal	33	16
Alternatives	8	25
Tactics	25	16
Strategy	16	16

Source: Dupont, 1982, p. 62.

The difference becomes even more marked if we see it alongside the relative amounts of time spent on goals: successful negotiators spend their time developing alternatives, while less successful negotiators chiefly engage in clarifying and refining intended goals and results. The difference in time spent on tactics is explained by the fact that successful negotiators limit themselves to an arsenal of opening moves; after that they rely on their ability to improvise: 'You can't predict exactly what course things will take; we can ask for a recess, or stall, if we have to.' Inexperienced negotiators tend to think up answers to obstacles that will not appear until later in the negotiating process, 'just in case'.

9.1 Checklist

The various aspects of preparation are presented here in the form of a checklist. This is not a list which must be followed to the letter: its object is to help the negotiator quickly enumerate possible points to be remembered, depending on the circumstances. The list can prevent him from forgetting a good move which he would have used if only it had occurred to him.

9.1.1 DIAGNOSIS

Contents

- Do we know enough about the matters to be discussed?
- Do we have the relevant documents and files?

- Do we know the history of the issue?
- Have we enlisted sufficient expertise on specialized aspects?
- Where do our interests and goals lie, where those of our opponents?
- Do certain premises/principles/policy statements have any bearing on these negotiations? What are ours, what are theirs?

Climate

- What sort of atmosphere do we expect at the negotiating table?
- Is a good relationship important for the future?
- Can we assess our own influence on the climate?
- What sort of people are we dealing with? What is their negotiating style, what is the 'story behind the story', what are they interested in personally?
- Can we keep interests and individuals separate?

Balance of power

- What are the strong and weak points of both sides?
- In what are we dependent on them, and in what are they dependent on us?
- If no agreement is reached, what are the consequences for both sides?
- Do we/they have alternatives available?
- Do we expect certain manipulations or other 'power plays'?
- What are the authorities of our opponents?

Constituency

- How strong is the position of our opponents towards their constituency? How strong is ours?
- Where do the primary interests of the constituency lie?
- What sort of mandate does the constituency give?
- Who are the opinion leaders in the constituency?
- With what sort of things that cost us relatively little can our negotiating partners score with their constituency (and vice versa)?
- Does the constituency constantly try to become involved in the negotiations, or is it clearly kept at a distance?
- To what extent do we/they need to put on a 'show' for the constituency?

9.1.2 GOALS

- What results do we want to obtain? What are our opponents aiming at?
- What is the very least we will be satisfied with?
- Is it possible and is it necessary to set down a dividing line between solutions that are just barely acceptable and solutions that are unacceptable? See figure 9.1.

Figure 9.1 Goals in negotiations

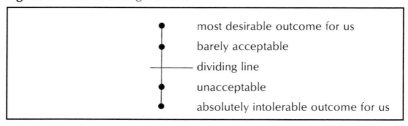

9.1.3 PROCEDURES

In order to increase flexibility, it is important to make the most of tactical and strategic opportunities in several areas. The following points can help here. They relate primarily to the outset of the negotiations. After that a checklist is not much help, at least not if one wants to remain flexible: one will have to improvise, call for a recess, or stall if difficulties arise.

Working with alternatives

- Have we utilized our informal contacts to exchange ideas and information?
- How open is our opening? Do we pin ourselves down immediately, or do we primarily give information about our underlying interests?
- Do we know enough about our opponents or do we need to draw them out some more, for example, by asking questions, playing dumb, showing an interest, waiting, setting a good example?
- How do we build up our line of reasoning? Do we have a story ready which makes it clear what our interests are?

- Have we expressed the results for which we are aiming in several alternatives? Have we succeeded in creating several options?
- Do we also try to increase flexibility at the negotiating table by preparing ourselves for procedures such as:
  - brainstorming, thinking out loud together, formulating tentative proposals;
  - enumerating, making inventories;
  - holding informal study groups;
  - adjourning;
  - cutting out discussions of who is right;
  - allowing tentative proposals to come on the table?

Tactical repertory of opening moves

Tactics relating to the content of the negotiations were mentioned in the previous section. Here we will distinguish tactical moves relating to the climate, balance of power and constituency.

Climate

- Can we work comfortably with the location and the arrangement?
- How informal do we want the climate to be? Points of attention are:
  - Are behaviour and clothing to be formal or informal?
  - Are first names to be used?
  - Will humour be prominent?
  - What opportunities will be taken to get to know one another somewhat better before the meeting, mixing informally?
  - Will there be informal conversation during coffee breaks?
  - Will lunch or dinner be taken jointly?
  - At the negotiating table, will the delegations be mixed around the table or will they be seated on opposite sides?
  - In the opening stages, should there be special attention to positive experiences shared, the continuity of the relationship, etc?
  - Might controversial members of the delegation be omitted or replaced?

Balance of power

- How will we deal with expected manipulations or other 'power ploys'?
- Where will they feel we are 'throwing our weight around'? Do we want them to?
- Will we work with a chairperson?

Constituency

- Will we manage to exert enough influence on our constituency to keep them at a distance? Points of attention are:
  - Is the location 'secluded' enough?
  - Is there sufficient time for preparatory contacts with constituency?
  - Will both sides spare each other a loss of face?
  - Will both sides allow each other moments of 'drama' which are well accounted for in the minutes?
  - Will both sides give up 20 per cent to allow the other side to score 80 per cent on certain points?

Strategic outline

There are four general strategic notions which can be useful during the preparations:

- scripts versus scenarios;
- phases of negotiations;
- negotiating styles;
- division of roles among delegation members.

Scripts versus scenarios: a strategic instrument with which we can increase our room to manoeuvre and to improvise is thinking in scenarios rather than scripts. Table 9.2 shows the script and the scenario side by side for easy comparison.

Phases: a second general notion which can offer some strategic grasp is that of the phases of negotiations:

- initial choice of position;
- exploratory phase;
- impasse and finalization.

Actions will need to be adapted to these phases. If they are not, negotiators make life unnecessarily impossible for themselves, for

Table 9.2 Script versus scenario

Script: one line of talk; rigid	Scenarios: several lines of talk, depending on the reactions; flexible
we start by saying . . .	we start by saying . . .
and then we bring up . . .	if they bring up . . .
along the way we also say . . .	then we point out that . . .
and only after they have admitted . . . do we bring up . . .	but if they right away say that . . .
until we have them at the point where . . .	then we . . .
etc.	etc.

example, by waiting too long with information about their own position, or by making a compromise proposal at too early a stage.

Negotiating styles: Some reflection about what emphasis we want to place in our negotiating style may be in order. For example, do we want to be

- directly confrontational?
- yielding, friendly?
- avoiding, passive?
- exploring?

Division of roles among delegation members: if the delegations each consist of more than one person, it is extremely important to clarify the division of roles in advance. Important points here are:

- Will we have one spokesperson?
- If not, what is the division of tasks?
- If so, when should we support or supplement him?
- Cultivate differences in style.

9.2 In conclusion

This 'checklist' contains many points. The art is to keep things simple. For example: quickly scan the checklist to pick out four items that appeal to you. Under each of them mark down a few terms that cover your points. Then try to work out your alternatives a little further. For the rest, rely on your ability to improvise; otherwise you can simply propose adjournment or think of something else.

Negotiators often have little time to prepare. When time is very limited, the following suggestions may help:

- appoint a delegation leader to preside; after having heard the delegation members, he settles matters;
- limit yourself to developing an opening in which you tell something about your interests and then play it by ear.

When time pressure is greatest, when you simply have to or want to arrive at a solution *immediately*:

- make a proposal which is as advantageous as possible but still well defensible;
- then barter until a reasonable compromise has been reached.

CHAPTER 10

Chairing Negotiations

Sometimes negotiations have a chairperson. At intra-organizational meetings of a negotiating character, it is often someone from a higher echelon; in other cases it may be an independent outsider. Sometimes the chair falls to one of the parties involved. The chairman may face a difficult task, particularly when the claims of the parties show great contrast, or in situations of competition for very scarce resources. This chapter provides a complete procedure for chairing meetings at which participants negotiate. The same procedure can be used in very diverse kinds of negotiations.

We assume that a chairman has two aims: he wants to reach a compromise; and he wants to reach it without impairing mutual relations. In order to achieve this dual purpose, he must both understand the phases in the negotiating process and develop procedural tactics to increase the chance of success. These two areas will be explored below.

10.1 The phases of the negotiating process

Knowledge of the phases of negotiating processes can serve a chairman in good stead. It will enable him to understand better what is taking place and to prepare himself better for what will come. Events become more predictable because he has a guiding principle. The four major phases, as discussed in earlier chapters, are:

- preparation;
- proclamations;
- psychological warfare;
- crisis and finalization.

In many types of negotiations, these phases take the much milder form:

- preparation;
- initial choice of position;
- search phase;
- impasse and finalization.

More information about the phases of negotiations can be found in chapter 8. Here we will briefly discuss these four phases, and the role of the chairman in each of them will be pointed out.

10.1.1 PREPARATION

In discussions among themselves, the parties determine their standpoints and the strategy to be adopted. The chairman is often not involved in these internal deliberations. If he is, he should try to keep both parties from committing themselves to one particular solution, asking about underlying interests and ultimate goals and encouraging each side to formulate several alternatives.

10.1.2 INITIAL CHOICE OF POSITION

Negotiations generally begin with statements in which the parties present their respective wishes and interests. On the basis of facts and arguments of principle (e.g. 'the company's objectives', 'the common interest'), they try to give their position some force. As chairman, it is important to give them the opportunity to do so without being interrupted by the other participants.

10.1.3 SEARCH PHASE

The parties test each other out. How reasonable are their claims? They also probe the interests and ideas in the background. The chairman must be alert to possible combinations of wishes and interests. Parties try to create as much leeway for themselves as possible in three ways:

- they try to keep open as many options as possible for themselves while giving up nothing;
- they test the tenacity of the other party;
- they look for possible combinations of interests.

In this phase proposals, sometimes still tentative, are put on the table. These proposals often imply concessions. A chairman can play a very important role here. He can encourage the parties to probe the 'integrative space' by having them present their underlying interests and assumptions. Even more important, he can prevent endless arguing by focusing the negotiations on concrete proposals. Finally, he can put a stop to vitriolic discussions.

10.1.4 IMPASSE AND FINALIZATION

Various proposals and counterproposals are on the table now. There is no agreement: all parties claim they have done their utmost. Time starts to press; tension rises. This creates more and more pressure to make decisions, to finalize matters. A few last concessions on both sides, sometimes combined in a clever package deal, can provide a way out at the last minute.

By wielding his authority, a chairman can sometimes settle certain points in this phase and thus facilitate a compromise. In this phase, too, a chairman can sometimes put a stop to 'fighting' behaviour, when people who are not particularly well equipped to deal with impasses become excessively rigid in their attitude and make excessive use of pressure. More experienced negotiators, however, see impasses as inevitable and sometimes even desirable, making mild test of the other's tenacity. They also give a powerful impetus to seek a more creative compromise which addresses better the various interests at stake.

10.2 Checklist for a chairman

The following checklist provides a series of procedural suggestions for chairmen.

1 Start with a brief explanation of:

- the object of the meeting;

- constraints (available time, consequences of failure to reach a decision);
- manner of decision-making (by consensus, by simple majority or by higher up);
- procedure (see the following points).

2 Give everyone the opportunity to clarify their wishes and interests:

- the magnitude of his wishes;
- precisely what those wishes imply;
- the why and wherefore: arguments, objectives, interests.

Do not allow any discussion yet – at most, a few questions to clarify matters. In particular, try to create leeway for clarification of the objectives and underlying interests; you may even ask about them yourself.

3 Briefly summarize wishes and interests.

4 Explore the 'integrative leeway' via common premises:

- investigate with the participants whether common premises and criteria can be found;
- try to chart common interests or objectives.

The search for common premises may cause problems. Often they prove to be too abstract to provide any sound footing. If this is the case, a better procedural step is the following:

5 Explore the 'integrative space' via proposals:

- make particular proposals, such as: allow only the highest priorities to be discussed; leave the situation as it is; lower all claims by 20 per cent; combine claims a and b; temporize all claims by 20 per cent; defer claims x and y;
- make a brainstorming inventory of as many alternative proposals and solutions as possible;
- turn participants' reactions into proposals for a solution;
- investigate whether proposals can be integrated by combining claims;
- take a proposal as a basis for further negotiating: avoid discussion of this proposal, ask for suggestions to improve it or for conditions on the basis of which one could agree to it;
- help participants to formulate amendments and conditions if necessary.

Exploring in this manner assumes a minimum of willingness to find a way out jointly. If it is successful, then it becomes clear via the proposals where everyone's primary interests lie. This often leads to a better result than does the system of bartering, item by item.

The fifth of these points deserves special emphasis: taking a proposal as a basis for further negotiating can be a very fortunate intervention by the chairman. Depending on the type of negotiations, this can vary from a draft text of a treaty to the tentative allocation of a budget. (This makes it theoretically possible to reduce the number of phases of the negotiation to two: a first 'start-up' phase, in which parties exchange information on the basis of which a tentative and broad but non-binding agreement is formulated, and a second phase in which the negotiations about the concrete substance move forward on the basis of that outline.) Then focus negotiations on this tentative proposal. This means restrict arguments and discussion. Ask instead for amendments or conditions which would make the proposal acceptable. This simple expedient gives the chairman a powerful tool with which to organize the negotiations more con-structively and to speed them up. Of all the procedural suggestions, this one is the most important!

6 Let the parties 'bicker' now and then. Some bickering is in-evitable and, to a certain degree, it is necessary to convince them that it is useless to go on talking in order to persuade and influence one another.

7 Let time pressure and rising tension do their work. At a certain point, although some concessions have been made, the matter is deadlocked. Time passes; the consequences of not reaching a decision loom large. The debating leads nowhere. The time is ripe to finalize the matter.

8 Carve out a decision: make a proposal for a compromise and give a brief but clear explanation.
A good compromise satisfies the following conditions:

- it gives some advantage to parties that have succeeded in linking their claims to generally acknowledged interests and goals;
- it gives expression to the current power and dependency relations;
- it exploits the integrative possibilities (for instance, a combina-tion of interests in a creative package deal);

- it leaves none of the parties behind in an isolated position or in the role of 'the big loser'.

10.3 Three final remarks

1 It is important for a chairman to put a stop to any tendency towards escalation. The following rules of thumb can be given for this:

- Cut off personal attacks and reprimand the assailant. People must keep the person and the issue separate. 'Don't blame your opponent for your problems.'
- Keep the parties in some sort of balance. Do not allow one party to be entirely thrust aside because of inexperience or a lack of coalition partners.
- Avoid discussions of principle. An appeal to higher values or generally shared interests can quickly lead to high-flown rhetoric and extensive debate. This has a rigidifying and polarizing effect, unless the principles are concretely applicable and the interests are truly common.

2 Do not expect the impossible! Especially when people and interests are mutually exclusive, in situations where all parties are going to have to give up something, it is impossible to expect that all parties can be fully satisfied. A smoothly running meeting is impossible. Harmony and consensus cannot be expected. To a certain extent, personal frustration and friction between participants is inevitable. But: *to a certain extent only*! For a chairman can definitely prevent escalation. A chairman has succeeded when parties can look back and see that they were given a fair chance: that they were in a position to come up tenaciously for their interests, and that continued discussions would not have led to a better outcome, but simply to time-consuming and fruitless bickering.

3 At such meetings, the biggest problem can be protracted arguing and debating. This yields no profit: people simply repeat the same arguments over and over. They feel called upon to 'explain matters once more' or to 'set misunderstandings straight', etc. The value of all these efforts is but slight; the effect is a rapid deterioration in the atmosphere towards the point where the participants start flea-picking, scoring points, etc. Sometimes negotiators are not well

aware of this. They really believe that there is still something to be explained or set straight; and they stop listening to their opponent, and merely rehearse their own argument for the next round!

The chairman can put a stop to this by keeping the discussion *focused on proposals*: what does one side want, what does the other side want; what allocation is proposed; on what conditions might the other side agree to it; what sort of compromise is conceivable? Only new arguments are still important at this point. The 'old familiar tales' only take time and arouse irritation.

10.4 Summary

We have described briefly the phases through which negotiations pass and have set out a checklist giving eight procedural suggestions aimed at facilitating the task of the chairman at meetings where participants negotiate with one another.

In this context three phases were distinguished as requiring particular kinds of intervention from the chair:

- initial choice of position, when the wishes and interests of the participants are presented; here suggestions 1, 2, and 3 are appropriate.
- search phase, when the parties explore the integrative space and test the tenacity of each other's positions; suggestions 4, 5, and 6 are useful here;
- impasse and finalization, when the matter seems to be dead-locked but a compromise proposal at the right moment shows a way out; suggestions 7 and 8 can be put into practice here.

CHAPTER 11

Negotiating with a More Powerful Party

11.1 Tendencies in situations of differential power

Power differences between parties affect behaviour. They can set in motion dynamics of their own which have an escalating effect; for example, when the less powerful party is driven further and further into a corner, and adopts either an aggressive or an apathetic attitude.

This chapter will first describe the *tendencies* in negotiations between more and less powerful parties. Table 11.1 shows:

- the problems that each side often faces with respect to the other;
- the behavioural tendencies on both sides which lead to serious escalation;
- the images that parties gradually develop of each other;
- the tactics which parties tend to adopt in order to maintain their own position.

These tendencies are summarized in diagrammatic form in figure 11.1. They can result, if unchecked, in lasting impasses or unmanageable confrontations.

The second half of the chapter will go into an *effective negotiating strategy for the less powerful party*.

Table 11.1 Outline of the tendencies in 'more versus less powerful' situations

	High power level	Low power level
Central problems	How can we keep things under control? How do we get across what has to be done? How can we prove it is fair? How do we promote acceptance? How do we deal with resistance? How do we find out what people think?	How do we avoid being taken in, committing ourselves to things we do not want? Can you really speak your mind freely? Won't they get back at you later? Is the matter still open? Do we really have all the information? Will we be called obstructionists?
Behavioural tendencies	Little willingness to take new developments into consideration. 'We have done all we can.'	Overestimate the rationality of the other party. Often find it very difficult to offer good opposition. Frequently exhibit long-lasting internal division.
	Superior attitude: 'Why so much distrust, we are aware of our responsibilities'.	React to contacts with the arrogant establishment with indignation and aggression.
	Tendency to derision, rigidifying into grimness. 'This is simply going too far, they ought to be put in their place.'	Close ranks. Tendency to provocation and to militant action.
	Tunnel vision: 'We have their interests at heart, but there is no way to get through to them. If they don't want to listen, they'll just have to find out the hard way.'	Tunnel vision: 'We can only make things any better by fighting. The whole system is rotten.'
Image of the other	Inflexible, suspicious. Not very creative: 'Nothing will come of it.' Think only of their own interests.	Manipulating, calculating: 'They'll have it their own way after all.' 'They know more than they tell you.' 'They always think of themselves first.'

Table 11.1 cont.

	High power level	Low power level
Examples of strategies	Persuading. Setting down consultation procedures. Influencing opinion leaders. Coercion: 'You can't please them all.' Letting complaints or proposals from lower echelons bog down in red tape. Stigmatizing and isolating resistance.	Refusing to take active part, withholding information. Keeping agreements purposely vague. Find a safe haven for their interests (in workers' council or unions). Passive resistance: let matters drag on, constant criticism of details. Ask for more information. Act injured, turn it into a matter of principles. Evade control, mobilize active resistance.

Figure 11.1 Dynamics of power differences

More powerful		Less powerful
Cajolery		Dependent, yielding
Persuasion	VERSUS	Aggressive
Coercion		Apathetic, passive

11.2 Strategic tips for the less powerful party

11.2.1 IN GENERAL

First and foremost, do not allow yourself to be bullied by your constituency. Study table 11.1 to see where and how this danger arises, with accusations of mistreatment, appeals to 'matters of principle', stereotyping the opponent.

11.2.2 SPECIFIC POINTS

- Make clear and specific proposals.
- Continue to ask questions about the difficulties and the costs that the more powerful party will face if they go ahead with their own proposals.
- Show explicit willingness to tackle these problems with the more powerful party and to keep the costs as low as possible for them. From an emotional point of view, this tactic can be very unsatisfying, because 'we are right in the final analysis' or 'what the other side wants is just plain crazy'. It is much more gratifying to nag, to appeal to principles, to go along with your constituency, etc. But this only further impairs your negotiating position!

With increasing influence:

- undertake calculated fighting to improve your strategic position;
- state at their most extreme the consequences of not reaching a compromise;
- mobilize the constituency in demonstrative actions to show potential power.

With decreasing influence:

- stall, postpone, adjourn;
- take the initiative, make detailed proposals.

Van Reekum and Segers (1986) came up with several suggestions in this area. Three of them are:

- assume there is agreement and work out the details together;
- offer alternatives to choose from;
- turn objections into conditions.

11.2.3 IMPORTANT POINTS

- Be careful about setting a bottom line to your own wishes if you cannot substantiate it. A bottom line has a restrictive effect: it forms an obstacle to exploring the negotiating leeway.
- Try to develop an *alternative* for not reaching a compromise.
  - What happens if no compromise is reached?

○ What can we do if no compromise is reached?

○ Specify the most promising ideas and make them feasible.

However difficult this may be, it is the only way to bring your own position more into balance. As long as there is no alternative, you are still in the position of underdog or victim. Remember: good alternatives seldom grow on trees. They must sometimes be developed with great effort. Try, too, to imagine the alternative for the other party of not reaching a compromise.

• The greater the power difference, the wiser it is to set down as many as possible *common* criteria and to negotiate from them. The more common norms, premises, criteria, etc., that can play a role in the negotiations, the better. So again: explore! What do we have in common, where are the underlying interests?

CHAPTER 12

From Fighting to Negotiation

It's all or nothing.
The best defence is attack.
It's a win-or-lose situation.
An eye for an eye, a tooth for a tooth.
If they don't want to listen, they'll just have to find out the hard way.
The first blow is half the battle.

How can we induce an opponent who uses a fighting strategy to negotiate? After a brief analysis of fighting behaviour, we will point out in this chapter several ways of dealing with it.

12.1 Fighting behaviour

A fighting strategy is concerned with achieving dominance and reducing the opponent to submission. In all possible ways, one party tries to gain ascendancy over the other in order to win. Examples of fighting behaviour are:

- causing damage, loss and inconvenience by action such as demonstrations, boycotts, strikes and sit-ins;
- emphasizing negative aspects in one's image of the opponent;
- sowing dissent;
- not listening, nagging, steamrollering;

- casting doubt on the competence and motives of the opponent and ridiculing him;
- flouting procedures, rules, norms and agreements;
- employing shock effects, personal attacks, threats, humiliation, flattery, angry outbursts until the opponent starts to make mistakes;
- trying to isolate the opponent, managing to find support everywhere for your own viewpoint and to invoke public disapproval of the opponent;
- purposely spreading false information;
- creating as much confusion, uncertainty and inclarity as possible;
- rushing or endlessly dragging out decision-making;
- working the opponent into an inferior position by barking rudely at him, disagreeing with him before he even opens his mouth, only hearing things which you can use against him, etc.

12.1.1 ADVANTAGES

A fighting strategy has a highly mobilizing and activating effect on one's own party; it can also be very satisfying emotionally.

- If a party is not very dependent on his opponent, he often stands to gain more by fighting than by negotiating.
- Internal differences are settled, the ranks close, the leaders are attributed larger powers.
- If one party clearly has superior power, it can be a quick way of settling a conflict.
- For a party which has not yet gained recognition, fighting for a while can be a manner of being taken seriously at the negotiating table.

12.1.2 DISADVANTAGES

- Distortions in the perception of the opponent; the 'bad' side is accentuated more and more heavily, while the 'good' elements are squeezed out of the picture.
- A continual negative effect on trust; the loser is constantly bent on revenge; subsequent sharp conflicts are likely.
- The less skilful or the less aggressive 'fighters' leave the scene, which can mean the loss of an important potential of energy and creativity.

- In the heat of the battle, people tend to lose sight of what the conflict is all about, as well as the consequences. Everything, sometimes even their own interests, has to give way to 'win' from the opponent. This is a very serious disadvantage.

It is extremely difficult to induce an opponent who uses a fighting strategy to adopt another strategy. Even worse, faced with a fighter, people tend to switch to a fighting strategy themselves, so that further escalation is to be expected: 'The opponent is playing hard, so we will play hard too'. It is doubtful whether self-interest is served in this way. In order not to slip *unintentionally* into fighting, it is important to have alternatives.

12.2 Possible ways of dealing with fighting behaviour

One thing these possibilities all have in common is that they stand a chance only if you prepare yourself well for them. Preparing and planning for this or that is a first requirement. In the second place, it is always important to be aware that you will feel a certain tendency in yourself, and probably clear pressure from your constituency, to play it tough. The best way to remain in control of this tendency is to have *clear goals of your own*. In a confrontation, if you have your own interests clearly in mind, if you know what it is you want to achieve, you can gauge any action you might want to take against this. It also makes it somewhat easier to compare the costs of a continuing fight with the costs of a negotiating situation.

The following tactics can be used:

- Try to find out what is behind the fighting behaviour of the opponent.
- Sidestep the fight. It takes two to quarrel; if one ignores the matter, it all stops.
- Maintain your position as imperturbably as possible. This often leads to an impasse. For the opponent, this may be a reason to start tackling matters differently.
- Announce that you do not wish to negotiate in this way. Indicate the rules and conditions under which *you* wish to deal with the other.

The first of these courses involves four steps:

1 Become acquainted with the why and wherefore of the behaviour of the other party; not only the more substantial
business-like side – underlying problems and interests – but
also any possible socio-emotional irritations the other party
may feel.

2 Investigate your own role in the cause of the problems under
(1). The following things may come to light.

   o The opponent is following the 'party line', and you are being
     used as a test case or being made party to a much wider con-
     flict.
   o The opponent has several concrete wishes, but is afraid that
     they will not be achieved through discussion and negotia-
     tion. 'There's no point in talking to a stone wall.'
   o The opponent is simply 'showing off' for his constituency.
   o The opponent thinks he is dealing with a party that thinks in
     terms of 'win or lose', one that is looking for a fight.
   o The opponent fights to gain recognition as a serious
     negotiating partner.
   o The opponent feels slighted, manipulated, unjustly dealt
     with, etc., by the treatment of the other side.

3 Steps (1) and (2) often lead to the identification of the issues to
be negotiated. What do we want, what do they want?

4 Reach a compromise by negotiating.

CHAPTER **13**

The Negotiating Grid and Personal Negotiating Styles

The dilemma negotiators must tackle is one of mutual dependence and differing interests. The skilful handling of this dilemma demands a degree of versatility and a particular combination of cooperation and competition. This chapter describes a model to clarify several personal negotiating styles. Perhaps you will be able to recognize your own style, but remember that the effect of any style depends on the situation in which it is exercised: so perhaps the best style is to be adaptable, according to the circumstances. This is not always easy. Part of our behaviour is firmly ingrained; no one is 100 per cent flexible. This is one more reason to be aware of your own tendencies in negotiating situations: only then is it possible to adjust and adapt them.

13.1 Two types of behaviour

In characterizing negotiating styles, we will work with two dimensions of negotiating behaviour which are considered to be of central importance by practising negotiators as well as by researchers.

In the first place: how does a negotiator deal with the tension between cooperation and fighting? His style with respect to this dimension is determined by the extent to which his attitude and

actions embody an acknowledgement of interdependency and inter-
action, as opposed to a more aggressive and domineering attitude.
The vital significance of this behavioural polarity for negotiators has
been described in chapter 2. The two poles are shown schematically
in figure 13.1.

Figure 13.1 Negotiating behaviour: the 'cooperation–fighting' axis

Cooperation: yielding, jovial, personal, friendly, promotes a good atmosphere, ◄ — ► open, sensitive to arguments of others	*Fighting*: stubborn, aggressive, scoring points, coercion, desire to dominate, calculating, makes self-interest primary

In the second place: how explorative is a negotiator? An active
attitude aimed at procedural flexibility in the search for solutions is of
central importance. Some negotiators search persistently for solutions that are relatively satisfactory for both parties. This can be done
without falling into the trap of making concessions. *Be firm but
flexible*! To achieve this, an extensive exchange of information is
needed – more particularly, trying out possible solutions in the form
of tentative suggestions, thinking out loud, informally sounding out
the other. Any possible integrative potential will then be fully
exploited. Making concessions would only lessen the impetus in this
direction.

The basic concept behind all this is interdependence. Parties are
negotiating because they are interdependent; interdependence
implies shared interests. So try to make the common good as tangible
as possible. The two poles of this behavioural axis are shown in
figure 13.2.

Figure 13.2 Negotiating behaviour: the 'flexible–avoiding' axis

Flexible: exploring, seeking background information and possible alternatives	*Avoiding*: passive, staying on one track, repetitive, detached, rigid

To understand this polarity, it is important to realize that one can
be passive in an ostensibly active manner. This can take the form of

repeating the same arguments in many different ways, sticking to one's original premises and rejecting new information, defending a particular solution through thick and thin, or making the issue a question of some non-negotiable principle. Tactically, this behaviour may sometimes be effective, as long as the person using it is aware that it is an entrenchment and thus puts a stop to the search for integrative potential, at least temporarily. It may take place very actively and vociferously, but it is in fact an avoidance of the search towards a compromise.

Each of the four poles identified on these two dimensions stands for a certain negotiating style.

- *Fighting*. Pursuing his self-interest at the expense of the other's. This style is often focused on power, and the fighter will resort to all available weapons – expertise, rank, financial sanctions – in order to win. Fighting can come in the guise of 'assertiveness' or of defending a standpoint because 'you are right'.
- *Cooperating*. In situations of opposed interests, this often leads to yielding. An important element of this style may be the perceived necessity to keep personal relations good above all else.
- *Avoiding*. Refusing to take on the confrontation. Avoidance can take the form of diplomatic evasion, postponement, stubbornly sticking to one track 'as a matter of principle', or simply evading the entire situation.
- *Exploring*. Trying to find a solution that satisfies the interests of both the parties involved as much as possible. This means studying a subject to identify the underlying interests and exploring alternatives that satisfy them.

We often see mixed forms of the various styles; below we will discuss four of them.

13.2 Four negotiating styles

Combining the two dimensions gives us the grid in figure 13.3, which will help to describe negotiating styles. To give a more detailed picture of how negotiating styles can be characterized, figure 13.4 and table 13.1 elaborate four examples.

Table 13.1 Personal negotiating styles

	Analytical–aggressive	Flexible–aggressive	Ethical	Jovial
Productive aspects	Careful analysis. Preference for hard facts and figures, sound logic. Weighs all alternatives ahead of time. Reliance on sound procedures. Keeps things predictable. Holds firmly on to goals	Wants to get things done; likes accomplishment. Likes to organize and energize others. Takes advantage of opportunities. Quick to act, likes challenges. Able to stand high level of tension; keeps things on the move, comes up with new ideas	Trust and belief in common values. Sets high standards. Independent thinking, sticks to principles. Develops proposals in the common interest. Considerate, helpful, dedicated. Often a 'bridge' between two parties	Socially skilled, personal charm, diplomatic. Tries to influence the climate positively. Eager to try things out, sensitive to integrative solutions. Flexible
Less productive aspects when used in excess	Over-preoccupation with details, no ability to improvise. Not sensitive enough to the climate of the discussions	Bossy, gives others too few chances. Easily becomes impatient and impulsive	Becomes 'preachy'. Overly concerned with ideals and common values to the point of being unrealistic	Offers too little resistance. Reluctant to take a stand, becomes ambivalent
Tendencies in a conflict	Amasses more and more 'evidence' that he is right; becomes stubborn	Does not concede, even when he knows he is wrong. Becomes angry, tends to coercive pressure. Tries everything within his power to win his case	Sticks to his case because he is 'right' or gives in, disappointed. Becomes disillusioned, is set apart	Overcompromising. Gives in to preserve harmony and good will

Figure 13.3 Negotiating styles

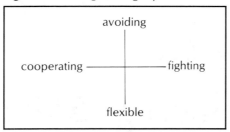

Figure 13.4 Elaboration of negotiating styles

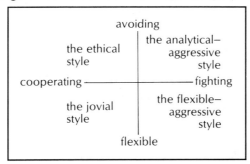

13.3 Conclusion

Your personal negotiating style is only one element in the negotiating game. Experienced negotiators know how to adapt their style to a particular situation, or to the means which are available to them at the moment, their relation to their constituency, the phase in which the negotiations are, the personalities of their opponents, etc.

How such factors can influence negotiating has been described in earlier chapters. A certain awareness of your own tendencies in the matter of style and an ability to vary them seem to me the best aims in this field. A style that (a) expresses the mutual dependency, (b) is tenacious as to goals and (c) is active in gathering information, exploring alternatives, and so on, is potentially ideal.

CHAPTER 14

Negotiating: Some Rules of Thumb

The following is a collection of tactics and rules of thumb recommended by experienced negotiators.

14.1 Time

Time is a very important factor in negotiations. People need time to get accustomed to new things. Resistance and opposition to a new proposal are natural: people not only need to be convinced by arguments, but also, and sometimes mainly, need time to reconcile themselves to it. Parties often begin negotiations with unrealistic goals and premises: negotiating can sometimes be a rude awakening. Wishes and illusions cannot be abandoned between one moment and the next. Patience can be an important factor in negotiations. With patience, you can consciously allow time to work for you.

Time limits and time pressure are part of negotiations. Always try to make time pressure work in your favour.

- Do not accept any time pressure from your constituency.
- Be alert to time factors that are important for your opponents, for example, certain conferences at which they will want to show results, vacations, holidays, etc.
- If your opponent has all the time in the world, take more time yourself.

- Be sceptical about deadlines that others impose on you. It almost always turns out to be possible to postpone them.
- Take care that you do not set yourself a psychological time limit. We all plan, but do not allow a schedule to be a noose that you draw around your own neck.

Time limits have a hypnotic effect. We tend to accept them even if we do not want to. This is why it is a good idea to link a proposal to a schedule as often as possible. It helps the other person to make the decision that you want him to make. Time limits work even when they ought not to.

14.2 Impasses

Most people are afraid of impasses. They are frustrating; they make us feel thwarted and helpless, while tension is clearly rising. Impasses are inevitable now and then in negotiations. They can be consciously used as a tactical weapon which may well take the form of coercion. An impasse tests the tenacity and the strength of the other party. It is also a means of generating new information or looking for alternative solutions.

Manners of breaking out of an impasse are:

- adjourning temporarily;
- giving a summary or overview of the various standpoints;
- making a small concession or suggesting that you will do so;
- exploring together the various alternatives and their respective consequences for the parties if the impasse continues;
- changing the composition of the delegation;
- changing the location;
- making an altered proposal;
- postponing the part of the negotiations that is causing difficulties until later;
- calling in a third party;
- calling for informal study;
- picking out a small part of the package and reaching agreement about that;
- systematically setting down the solutions once again;
- becoming emotional or starting to threaten if someone flares up;

- picking a key figure from the other delegation either to placate or to put under pressure;
- postponing negotiations;
- setting up a joint committee.

14.3 Questions and answers

It is very difficult for some people to give an answer to a question quickly and accurately. If you are one of these, the best solution is to think up and write down in advance all questions that might possibly be asked. Remember that some questions do not deserve an answer. The more time you have to think over a question, the better your answer will be. Suggestions in this context are:

- never answer before you fully understand the question; ask the other party to clarify it;
- remember that you can give an answer that goes into only a part of the question;
- a way of avoiding questions is to answer one that was not asked;
- some questions can be shelved because insufficient information is available to answer them.

Questions are eye-openers. They promote information exchange and understanding between parties. The shortest way to understanding is a good question. Suggestions for asking questions are:

- do not ask antagonistic questions;
- do not ask questions that criticize the honesty of the other; it won't make him any more honest;
- don't forget to listen in your desire to ask a question; write the question down and wait for the right moment;
- make sure you have formulated your question ahead of time;
- have the courage to ask questions that pry into other people's affairs;
- have the courage to ask dumb questions;
- have the courage to ask questions that will be avoided; the answer may provide exceptional information;
- recess often enough to formulate new questions;
- be persistent in asking questions if the answer is evasive or poor.

Answers that are not answers include the following: would you repeat the question – I don't understand the question completely – it depends – that is an entirely different subject – you must understand the history; it all started . . . – before I answer, you should understand the procedure – I have no experience with that, but I have heard – it varies because – it is not a matter of yes or no, but of the extent to which . . . – let's be more specific – it is not exactly as you put it – it's a question of how you look at it – as I just said . . . – sometimes things just go that way . . .

14.4 Adjourning

The effectiveness of negotiating increases if many adjournments are asked for; it makes more sense than long meetings and short breaks. Negotiating is not a ping-pong game in which each stroke must be answered immediately. Ask for time and use it to consult with your own people; you need it to:

- oversee what they have heard;
- think over questions;
- develop new arguments;
- explore new alternatives;
- discuss possible concessions;
- consult experts;
- check rules and agreements (procedures);
- study changes in circumstances or conditions;
- anticipate troublesome questions;
- develop new questions yourself.

14.5 The goal

The higher the aspiration level, the better the results. People who set a higher goal and oblige themselves to make efforts to reach it achieve more. There is a risk inherent in this: an impasse. Despite this risk, if you aim higher, you come out better.

Do remain realistic, however. Occupying extreme negotiating positions or offering a little extra for no apparent reason will do your reputation no good. It arouses the impression that you are not to be taken seriously, that your credibility is low. A good rule is: do not ask anything that you cannot defend with facts and arguments; start with the highest *defensible* bid.

14.6 Concessions

- Give yourself negotiating leeway; start high, but never higher than you can substantiate with arguments;
- let the other party make the first concession on an important matter, while you take the initiative on less important points;
- save your own concession; the longer the other party has to wait, the more he will appreciate it;
- tit-for-tat concessions are not necessary; if the other gives sixty, you can give forty; if he says, 'Let's split the difference,' you can always say, 'I can't.'
- don't be afraid to say no; if you say no several times, the other party will stop asking;
- don't be afraid to retract a concession made earlier;
- make a concession that gives away nothing.

Concessions that cost nothing are:

- an undertaking to consider it;
- assuring the other that, although you might want to, you simply cannot;
- showing that other competent and respected persons have made the same choice;
- giving as thorough an explanation as possible.

14.7 Agenda

Whoever controls the agenda controls what comes up and, more importantly, what does not come up for discussion. An agenda provides initiative; after all, it is a plan for discussion. Talk about the agenda before the negotiations start.

- Do not simply accept an agenda from the other party without thinking through the consequences.
- Look to see where and how your own topics can best be introduced.

- Study any agenda formulated by the other party for significant omissions.

14.8 Power of persuasion

14.8.1 KNOW YOUR FACTS

- Know the history, the organization and the person with whom you will negotiate;
- have the courage to ask the other to describe his authority or area of competence;
- know the organizational structure of the other party;
- know all the necessary documents.

14.8.2 PAY ATTENTION TO YOUR PRESENTATION

- How do you sit (not nonchalant, but not too tense either)?
- look at those present;
- structure what you say (be ordered, simple, concise);
- use the equipment available (for example, the flipover);
- pause for breath, do not rattle on.

14.8.3 ADOPT A CONSTRUCTIVE ATTITUDE WITHOUT GIVING IN

- It is better to start with subjects on which agreement can easily be reached than with controversial issues;
- agreement on controversial issues is easier to reach if they are linked to matters on which it is fairly simple to reach agreement;
- acceptance increases when the similarities are emphasized more than the differences;
- agreement is more readily reached when there are common interests to be discovered;
- bring forward tentative summaries and conclusions yourself rather than leaving it to the other party.

14.8.4 LIMIT YOURSELF IN YOUR ARGUMENTS

The more arguments you bring up, the greater is the chance that the other party finds one among them that he can cut down. Your other arguments are contaminated by this weaker point. The experienced negotiator is selective in the use of his facts and continually asks himself how and when he can present them as convincingly as possible. He makes sparing but persuasive use of printed information (reports, texts of laws, statistics, etc.).

14.8.5 LIMIT YOURSELF IN DEBATING

Sometimes negotiations deteriorate into almost endless debating: people merely repeat the same arguments over and over. They feel called upon to explain matters yet again and to straighten out 'misunderstandings', etc. The value of all these efforts is minimal: they are far more likely to worsen the climate. A good way to put a stop to this is to make a proposal and to keep the discussion aimed at proposals: what does one party want, what does the other want? On what conditions might a party be able to agree to a proposal? What compromises are conceivable? Only new facts and arguments are important. The 'old familiar tales' only waste time and arouse unnecessary irritation.

CHAPTER 15

Emotional Manipulations in Negotiations

Negotiations are always about something substantial: personnel, budgets, division of authority, tasks. In addition to this substance, there is also the aspect of the personal relationship between the participants. Negotiators conduct themselves towards each other in various ways: they show more or less openness, friendliness, malice, arrogance, restfulness. In this way they influence the *climate*. During negotiations, participants make all kinds of remarks and comments, sometimes spontaneous and intuitive, sometimes purposeful and calculating, which evoke certain feelings and incite responses from their opponent. These negotiators do not need to indicate openly what their true intentions are with such statements; they may even be in contrast to their actual opinions. Sometimes such remarks are intended to influence the *balance of power*.

15.1 Negative and positive manipulations

A party may let it be known to his opponent that the latter's views and behaviour simply do not come up to the mark, that they deserve only disapproval. The opponent is given to understand that his opinion is in fact somewhat short-sighted, that his reasoning is not logical, that he would do well to adopt a more constructive attitude, that his ideas and premises no longer work in these modern times, that his argument is devoid of principles. But negotiators may also observe that their opponents have formulated a thorough and innovative report, that they are well known for their progressive thinking, that their premises should be the basis of any further discussion, and that their contribution can be viewed as highly constructive. These negative and positive remarks often do not express the negotiators' true opinions; they may even express precisely the opposite! In this case, we call them *manipulations*.

Why do negotiators use manipulations? The object is to evoke certain feelings in the opponent, feelings that will lead to a strengthening of the manipulator's own position in the negotiations. In the case of *negative* manipulations, the aim is to evoke feelings of inferiority, of a sense of guilt, of being publicly disapproved of, in the other. Take, for example, an accountant who tells his client that a modern businessman cannot avail himself of this sort of financial misrepresentation. Or a manager who announces to his employee that his form of reporting is not compatible with the awareness of responsibility that prevails in the company. Or a union negotiator who lets the employers know that their attitude will damage labour relations for years to come. A person who uses negative manipulations hopes that his opponent will start to waver, become uncertain, yield.

If a person uses *positive* manipulations, he is buttering up his opponent in an effort to induce him to take a more compliant attitude. The accountant above might say to the businessman that his small fiscal irregularities would cast an unnecessary slur on his refreshingly progressive and innovative company policy. And the manager could tell his employee that his report was a clear improvement on the previous one, and that incidentally . . . And the union negotiator might say that the attitude of the employers fits well into the pattern of current labour relations, that it would lead to improved understanding on both sides, and that if the employers would simply make a change on one small detail, then . . .

15.2 Are emotional manipulations effective?

Do negotiators achieve what they want to achieve with their manipulations? Do they make the other party more yielding and more compliant?

An experienced negotiator will take little notice of manipulations. He will see through them and know that they are part of the game. If his opponent uses exaggerated positive manipulations, they are sometimes taken as humourous, and humour has a relaxing effect in negotiating discussions. However, if his opponent frequently uses negative manipulations, they are likely to arouse a feeling of irritation, not so much because he takes the accusations to heart, but in annoyance at the negotiating style, by the manner of the opponent. Apparently he has to deal with a negotiating partner who understands so little of the trade that he feels he must make use of insinuations. The behaviour of the manipulating negotiator will turn against him: instead of creating compliance, he creates irritation, resentment and intractability.

An inexperienced negotiator is more likely to allow himself to be influenced by manipulations in the talks. If his opponent has such a positive opinion of them, surely he will offer something for it in return? He feels flattered and above all wants to make sure that progress in the negotiations is not impeded. That is, until he gets back to his constituency, where he hears that the concessions he has made are absolutely unacceptable, that he is not fit to negotiate, and that he must try to retract those concessions. It is then that it begins to dawn on him that he has allowed himself to be taken in by sweet talk. The feeling of flattery turns into rancour and antipathy.

It is even more difficult for an inexperienced negotiator to deal with negative manipulations. If his opponent calls him unreliable, destructive or unbusiness-like, as if it is something everyone takes for granted, they cannot shrug it off. He gets the feeling that, if he is judged so negatively on the basis of such fundamental and generally recognized standards of decency, there must be something wrong with him: and so he starts to fell uncertain, to hesitate, to doubt. And perhaps to give in. Feelings of irritation crop up below the surface. He feels as if the rug is being pulled out from under his feet. Somewhere something is wrong: but what? How can a person defend himself?

Figures 15.1 and 15.2 show the intended and unintended effects of emotional manipulations: they are of a wide variety. In the end, emotional manipulations usually defeat themselves. Instead of compliance, they bring about intractability.

Figure 15.1 Negative emotional manipulations

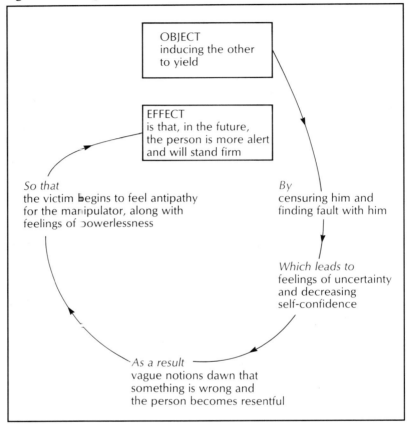

15.3 Opposition to manipulations

Emotional manipulations do not work, at least not in the long run. One might, perhaps, gain short-term success by using them on less experienced negotiators; in the end, however, the climate is damaged and the atmosphere is impaired. Often negotiating talks are rooted in wider-reaching and more complex transactions in which it is desirable or even necessary to keep relations between the parties positive. How, then, is one to deal with a manipulating opponent? Responding with manipulations, especially negative ones, only leads to

Figure 15.2 Positive emotional manipulations

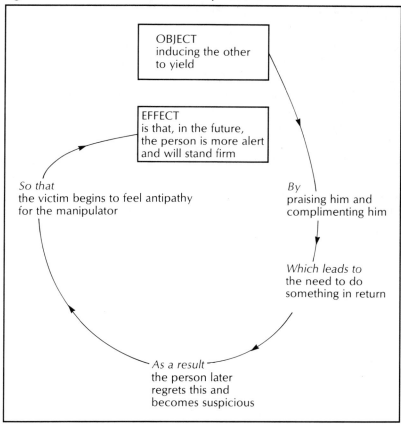

further polarization. What more constructive reactions can one make?

Recognizing manipulations, having a clear view of the actual intentions of the opponent and the manner in which he tries to achieve them, is already a very important point. Then you can take the behaviour of the other for what it is and simply not engage with it. Even simply labelling a word, a sentence or an argument an 'emotional manipulation' for yourself can be of help. If the other party insists and forces you to reply to the manipulation, you can restate your own interests and goals in a friendly tone. Reactions that impair the climate of the talks are: producing proofs that the other is wrong, indignantly rejecting the insinuation, ridiculing his opinions.

The most fundamental defence against emotional manipulations is becoming aware of your own feelings of being threatened, of aggression and inferiority. I once met a negotiator who became quite enraged at allusions by his opponent to his appearance (opponent: 'And then those spruce gentlemen from that company come in, and that's what I have to do business with . . .'). After a little searching, it appeared that the irritation of this man sprang from the fact that his family had been poor in his youth, and that his manner of presenting himself was still a reaction to that period of poverty. Manipulations by his opponent were successful when they alluded to this. Here we are almost into the field of depth psychology – but who doesn't have weak points arising from the past? Investigating what sort of manipulations make us feel most injured can be a help.

CHAPTER 16

Negotiating Inside Organizations: From Vertical Control to Horizontal Monitoring

Negotiating assumes that there is a certain relationship between negotiating partners. The characteristics of such a relationship are:

- relatively strong mutual dependence;
- pronounced self-interest on each side;
- no clearly superior power on one side or the other.

If we look at organizational structures in companies and organizations, how can the relations between their various units be characterized? To what extent do they exhibit these three characteristics?

The classical organizational structure, still very common today, is the pyramid. Similar duties are clustered into functional individual units. This functional division of labour over separate units and services is often carried to extremes. Coordination and control are strongly hierarchical. This last point in particular can mean less leeway for negotiating between units: so much is decided and regulated by higher echelons that there is nothing left to negotiate. Units have little individual independence and concentrate each on only one facet of production; this makes for less pronounced self-interest. There is still a certain amount of leeway for negotiation, but the organizational structure in itself is not conducive to it.

Recently a different organizational form has been gaining in popularity increasingly widely. The basic principles of this organizational form are the following.

- Structure the organization in well-defined units with clear responsibilities of their own, including responsibility for profit. These units should each focus on an integral product and not on any one functional aspect or specialism. It often turns out to be possible to integrate certain staff activities in such a unit.
- Make it possible for units to stand out from each other. This is usually accomplished by providing quick feedback on certain measurable performance indicators such as productivity, quality or costs. Continual comparison on these indicators with similar units inside and outside the organization is another frequent method. Sometimes a system of bonuses is linked to favourable results.
- Make it easy for employees to identify with the unit, for example, by giving them relatively large responsibilities, their own budgets, the freedom to tackle things in their own way and to experiment; by promoting team spirit and a feeling of solidarity; by an informal atmosphere and good personal relations. This stimulates motivation and vitality of units; to balance this, the structure should also be reinforced in another way.
- Ensure horizontal mobility (this point is very strong and very successfully applied in Japanese companies!). This creates generalists and all-round managers with an overview of the whole. It makes the network of interdependencies more manifest and keeps mutual rivalries mild. Horizontal job rotation is particularly important for the management of staff departments and other services whose results are harder to measure. Too often they contain established strongholds of managers who have made themselves invincible in their field. In this situation a client orientation and providing service to other organizational units tend to become more and more secondary to the primary purpose of consolidating and strengthening their own established position.
- Stimulate the 'we-feeling': a colourful tradition, achievements that lend prestige and command the respect of society, joint activities, comparison with last year's performance or with the competition are all opportunities for this.

What is coming into focus is more decentralized, federalist organizational form. It aims to cultivate relatively independent units, preferably each bearing responsibility for its own profitability, and preferably with a few simple output criteria on the basis of which steering is possible. Staff departments, too, can be enabled to develop in this direction by setting up transfer pricing agreements for their services and/or by giving them an opportunity to offer their services on the free market. It is interesting to note that a great vitality is ascribed to such organizational forms because they appeal directly to the adaptability, the creativity and the enthusiasm of the employees.

This organizational form is highly sophisticated. It is important to realize that *hierarchical steering and control* are largely replaced by *horizontal monitoring*. What remains is a management that controls along general lines. Units influence one another much more effectively through sharing and comparing results than management possibly could. It is a kind of monitoring that aims at results rather than functional prerogatives. In this way, competitive energy can be directly applied to achieving greater joint effectiveness. This kind of organizational form, with its positive effects on motivation and internal entrepreneurship, is not new, but recently it has been receiving much more attention, and is being put forward as the best way to increase productivity and competitive strength. Extensive studies of excellent organizations and comparison of successful Japanese and Western companies all point in the same direction (Pascale & Athos, 1981; Peters & Waterman, 1982; Ouchi, 1981). The crucial elements are:

- small, independent units with clearly delineated tasks, including tasks such as control and planning;
- dismantling top-heavy staff organs and bringing them closer to production;
- 'flattening' the organization, placing responsibilities at a lower level;
- less hierarchical and more horizontal pressure;
- investing in all possible ways in the development of personnel;
- a strong client orientation;
- horizontal mobility;
- rewards for achievements;
- making performance tangible, resulting in continual feedback and comparison.

There is a general feeling that organizations will simply have to carry out such changes – some of which are far-reaching – in order to survive. The competition for scarce resources and the need for a more integrated approach to problems can impel government as well as corporate and private organizations in the same direction. It is clear that this organizational structure has very distinct repercussions for all three of the relational characteristics mentioned at the beginning of this chapter, bringing

- very pronounced self-interests;
- strong mutual dependencies;
- less interference from above.

These are structural developments that can increase the need for constructive negotiating inside organizations.

It is interesting to see that the change in structure involves strengthening both the competitive and the cooperative impulses. For any individual unit, it emphasizes its independence, its results compared to those of other units and its internal cohesion. It is ingenious that these competitive forces between units can be combined with strong cooperative forces within the larger whole: presenting a united front, decision-making aimed at consensus and a strong we-feeling in the form of a company culture. The precise workings of this organizational form have been described in greater detail elsewhere (Mastenbroek, 1987). My impression is that it brings about a stronger balance of tension between units of *both* the forces towards each other *and* the forces away from each other. Some aspects of this balance of tension are shown in figure 16.1.

Figure 16.1 Relations as tension balances of both competitive and cooperative impulses

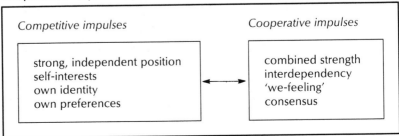

It is the balanced tension between competitive and cooperative impulses that promotes the vitality of the organization and the motivation of the employees. To maintain the correct equilibrium a certain skill in management is required. Too much emphasis on competition and the organization is 'torn apart', people feel insecure, aggressive action is too much encouraged. Too much cooperation and the organization becomes complacent, sluggish, loses its alertness; it may be quite a safe and secure haven for its employees, but it is also boring.

16.1 Examples

To give a better idea of the many sorts of situations in which negotiating skills are useful, a number of examples follow. The first two situations exemplify the 'successful' organizational structure described above. In all five cases, the object was to learn to cope better with contrasts inherent in the organizational structure. Except in the last example, managers were taught negotiating techniques tailored to their particular situations.

1 The regional offices of a banking firm became more autonomous. New systems brought the results of the individual branches into clearer view, promoting increasing competition for interesting clients in 'one another's regions'. In addition, a more independent attitude towards the head office developed, a trend further encouraged by the use of transfer pricing for the assistance and support from central staff departments. Polarized relations and delayed decision-making were foreseen.

In workshops, negotiating skills were taught. Simulations were used of practical situations of two types of frequently occurring tensions: region versus region and region versus head office.

2 Managers of profit centres of a retail company had a hard time finding a good basis for cooperation both in the stores and among themselves. Purchasing and sales had recently been combined; the new department was jointly responsible for the results. But classic frictions between purchasing and sales were still playing a role. The profit centres competed for budgets, space and other facilities. In a series of workshops, the problems were defined and negotiating skills were taught to resolve them.

3 Administrators of a large professional organization observed that negotiations with other interest groups, including government authorities, were becoming more and more tedious. Internal bickering was increasing. It took more and more effort to get the divergent interests inside the association under a common denominator. A third complication was the fact that the constituencies were growing more active. In several two-day conferences negotiating skills were taught and applied to specific situations.

4 A great many struggles for competence occur within and among some governmental agencies. Decisions are split up among a large number of authorities, each of which only oversees a single aspect of the problem. This is not very conducive to a smooth work flow or coordination. An attempt is being made to reach optimal solutions and workable compromises faster by teaching negotiating skills.

5 In a central workers' council, disagreement arose among the elected members from the various plants about the allocation of new jobs among the plants. According to a management plan, there was one plant that could count on expansion, while two other plants would have to give up jobs. Disagreement over this escalated so high that even fairly simple matters became contentious issues. Mistrust grew. Sharp reproaches and emotional accusations became the order of the day.

A consultant was enlisted; he decided to hold a confrontation meeting to reduce mistrust, and then, using a problem-solving model, to tackle the question it had all started with. The confrontation meeting took one day. Afterwards, people had mixed feelings about the result. Some of them called it a waste of time and wanted to 'get down to business'; others felt that things had been cleared up. According to the consultant, not much had changed. The mistrust hardly seemed less; only the intensity of the conflict had been reduced. This was due in part to an agreement about a cooling-off period during which the parties were not to undertake any further action in the matter.

The next session lasted two and a half days. The consultant started by explaining the problem-solving model which was to be the method of working for the rest of the conference. After a constructive start, on the morning of the second day the matter was completely deadlocked. Two diametrically opposed standpoints were at odds. The problem-solving model no longer worked; parties merely reiterated their standpoints. The atmosphere rapidly worsened.

Personal attacks and emotional accusations started. The consultant decided to leave the problem-solving model for what it was. He adjourned the meeting and asked the factions to consult among themselves on the crisis that had come about, particularly about the possible consequences if it were to continue.

The consultant had been probing in the wrong direction, but here he started to find the right tack. At issue was the distribution of scarce resources – jobs. From then onwards, his approach focused more and more on getting the parties to negotiate. Cultivating the crisis was a strong intervention; instead of worrying about the talks failing and undertaking an industrious search for compromises, he did something entirely different.

He had the parties investigate the consequences of a lasting crisis: a meeting prematurely broken off, continuing combat, animosity, resignation of several members, greatly decreased credibility of the elected members among their constituency, impaired influence on the management, etc. People were impressed by this and decided to try once more. The consultant asked the parties to set down conditions on the basis of which they could agree to a rough draft of a compromise. This use of a proposal as a platform for negotiations was decisive for the further course of the conference. The 'platform proposal' could be altered and amended in all possible ways. It put a stop to the endless arguments. All energy was concentrated on working out a concrete proposal. The consultant viewed the impasses occurring after this in the discussions (in fact, now *negotiations*) as legitimate pressure on one another's standpoints. He allowed them to continue until, generally after an adjournment, a concession set things in motion once again. In short, he worked with a typical negotiation approach. Ultimately the parties reached a compromise.

APPENDIX 1

Review of the Literature

This appendix contains a survey of the most important trends in the literature on negotiating and it provides a good starting point for further reading in the field. It does not pretend to be complete, but merely to give an impression of the various schools of thought. A number of titles are given in illustration of each approach.

The literature on negotiating comprises three main schools of thought:

1 Work intended for practical application.
2 Case studies.
3 More scientific work.

These three schools of thought will be discussed in sequence.

Work intended for practical application

These are books that contain directly applicable knowledge, primarily consisting of rules of thumb and tactical recommendations and usually illustrated with numerous brief examples. Well-known works are:

Calero, H. H., *Winning the Negotiation* (New York, Hawthorn Books, 1979).

Coffin, R. A., *The Negotiator: A Manual for Winners* (New York, Amacon, 1973).

Cohen, H., *You Can Negotiate Anything* (New York, Bantam, 1982).

Karras, C. L., *The Negotiating Game* (New York, Thomas Crowell, 1970).

Karras, C. L., *Give & Take: The Complete Guide to Negotiating Strategies and Tactics* (New York, Thomas Crowell, 1974).

Nierenberg, G. I., *The Art of Negotiating: Psychological Strategies for Gaining Advantageous Bargains* (New York, Hawthorn Books, 1968).

Nierenberg, G. I. and Calero, H. H., *How to Read a Person Like a Book* (New York, Hawthorn Books, 1971).

Ringer, J. J., *Winning through Intimidation* (Los Angeles, Los Angeles Book Publishers Co., 1973).

Scheerer, H., *Die Kunst erfolgreich zu verhandeln [The Art of Successful Negotiating]* (Kissing, Weka-Verlag, 1980).

Many of these works are slanted in a certain direction: the authors create an image of success; their work will make the reader a 'winner'. The cover of Cohen's book declares: 'the world's best negotiator tells you how to get what you want'. There is an undertone of firm self-assurance, aimed at scoring points on your neighbour, preferably without his knowing it or being able to do anything about it. Ringer beats them all: in addition to the revealing title, *Winning through Intimidation*, the blurb also states enticingly: 'read this book and start winning today'. The other books contain more references to the interdependency of negotiators and the necessity of adopting a 'win–win' strategy. Scheerer is the most extreme in this respect: in his book, the difference between harmonious cooperation and negotiation has become obscure.

Such books are made up of rules of thumb and practical tactics. Karras (1974), with over 200, is the most exhaustive. These books also contain many examples and anecdotal material, making them easy reading and earning them popular appeal: Cohen was listed on the *New York Times* 'best-seller list' for four months, Ringer for eight. It is fascinating fare, and it can definitely give one useful ideas. But it is so unsystematic as to limit its practicality. Where do you start with 200 pointers listed in alphabetical order? Even if you learn them by heart, how do you know in which situations each of the 200 is applicable? It is easy to miss the wood for the trees. These lists seem to ask to be subdivided into a limited number of related categories – into a model of negotiating that provides a sound basis, and practical indications of how to act.

Most books do classify tactics into a limited number of main categories. This helps a little; however, coherence and internal consistency often remain weak. In addition, the authors look to the behavioural sciences for a theoretical basis. The needs hierarchy of Maslow is popular with several of them; Scheerer uses transactional analysis. Karras (1970), in a particularly inventive attempt, uses a series of behavioural science models. But they are still too isolated; integration is lacking.

For the time being, this approach has reached its high point in the following two titles:

- Fisher, R. and Ury, W., *Getting to Yes* (Boston, Houghton Mifflin, 1981).

Because the authors restrict themselves to a limited number of basic instructions, their message comes across clearly. In addition, these two authors take a fairly remarkable starting point: negotiating must be based on principles and criteria: 'the method of principled negotiating'.

- Scott, W. P., *The Skills of Negotiating* (Aldershot, Gower, 1981).

Comprehensive and down-to-earth, with a comparatively large number of instructions which are well-organized.

Case studies

Many negotiators, especially politicians and diplomats, have put their experiences down on paper, producing altogether an abundance of literature. In sometimes very vivid language, these books give a good idea of how things can go behind the scenes. Examples are:

Abel, E., *The Missile Crisis* (New York, Bantam, 1963).

Dean, A. H., *Test Ban Disarmament; the Path of Negotiation* (New York, Harper & Row, 1966).

Golan, M., *The Secret Conversations of Henry Kissinger* (New York, Bantam, 1976).

Robertson, T., *Crisis: The Inside Story of the Suez Conspiracy* (New York, Atheneum, 1965).

Tanter, R., *Modeling and Managing International Conflict: The Berlin Crisis* (Beverly Hills, Calif., Sage, 1974).

Van Thijn, E., *Dagboek van een onderhandelaar* (Amsterdam, Van Gennep, 1978).

Zartman, W., *The 50% Solution* (New York, Anchor Press, 1976).

In some cases, the material was collected by a scientist or by a diplomat with scientific learnings. Such authors try to impose order and to make recommendations for others. The book by Zartman with the intriguing subtitle, 'How to bargain successfully with hijackers, strikers, bosses, oil magnates, Arabs, Russians and other worthy opponents in this modern world', is a good example. Other examples of authors trying to generalize on a range of experiences are:

Druckman, D., *Human Factors in International Negotiations: Social Psychological Aspects of International Conflict* (London, Sage, 1973).

Iklé, F. C., *How Nations Negotiate* (New York, Harper & Row, 1964).

Lall, A., *Modern International Negotiation* (New York, Columbia University Press, 1966).

Kaufmann, J., *Conference Diplomacy* (Dordrecht, Nijhoff Publishers 1988).

More scientific work

The scientific approach to negotiating has two main currents: detailed empirical studies, and the development of broad theories.

DETAILED EMPIRICAL STUDIES

An estimated 500 studies have been made of possible relationships in negotiating situations. The majority were performed by social psychologists; interested readers will find a number of these studies listed below. Their titles give a good impression of the types of questions which interested the researchers.

Aranoff, D. and Tedeschi, J. T., 'Original states and behavior in the prisoner's dilemma game', *Psychonomic Science*, 1968, 79–80.

Baron, R. A., 'Behavioral effects of interpersonal attraction: compliance with requests from liked and disliked others', *Psychonomic Science*, 1971, 325–6.

Benton, A. A., 'Bargaining visibility and the attitudes of negotiation behavior of male and female group representatives', *Journal of Personality and Social Psychology*, 1975, 661–75.

Benton, A. A., Kelley, H. H. and Liebling, B., 'Effects of extremity of offers and concession rate on the outcomes of bargaining', *Journal of Personality and Social Psychology*, 1974, 141–50.

Eisenberg, M. A. and Patch, M. E., 'Prominence as a determinant of bargaining outcomes', *Journal of Conflict Resolution*, 1976, 523–38.

Hornstein, H. A., 'The effects of different magnitudes of theat upon interpersonal bargaining', *Journal of Experimental Social Psychology*, 1965, 282–93.

Kelley, H. H. and Stahelski, A. J., 'The inference of intentions from motives in the prisoner's dilemma game', *Journal of Experimental Social Psychology*, 1970, 401–19.

Kogan, N., Lamm, H. and Tremonsdorf, G., 'Negotiation constraints in the risk-taking domain: effects of being observed by partners of higher or lower status', *Journal of Personality and Social Psychology*, 1972, 143–56.

Pruitt, D. G. and Drews, J. L., 'The effect of time pressure, time elapsed and the opponent's concession rate on behavior in negotiation', *Journal of Experimental Social Psychology*, 1969, 43–60.

Vidmar, N., 'Effects of representational roles and mediation on negotiation effectiveness', *Journal of Personality and Social Psychology*, 1971, 48–58.

Wall, J. A., 'Intergroup bargaining: effects of opposing constituent's stance, opposing representative's bargaining, and representative's locus of control', *Journal of Conflict Resolution*, 1977, 459–74.

Such studies exhibit several similarities.

- Relationships are represented statistically. To do so, negotiating behaviour is operationalized in quantitative parameters.
- An explanation for the relationships found receives comparatively little attention.
- It is unclear what we can do with the relationships. Although a few recommendations can be distilled from most studies, they

are usually valid only for very simplified negotiating situations. (One of the most commonly used research models is the 'prisoner's dilemma', a highly stylized game with only a few alternatives.)

- Other variables, and there are a great many of them, are kept constant. It is not clear what the findings are worth if such factors are allowed to vary.
- The most important drawback, however, is this: even if we were to take the 500 studies very seriously and even if we were to follow their recommendations, it would get us nowhere! The relationships they establish and the commendable ideas they propose are unwieldy in their sheer volume. There is no overall view, no internal consistency, no structure. Some scientists cherish the hope that all findings will one day fit together like the pieces of a puzzle. This hope is proving to be more and more in vain, although several laudable attempts have been made to do so. The following two books give a good idea of this.

- Morley J. and Stephenson, G., *The Social Psychology of Bargaining* (London, Allen & Unwin, 1977).
- Rubin, J. L. and Brown, B. R., *The Social Psychology of Bargaining and Negotiation* (New York, Academic Press, 1975).

In themselves, both books are clever compilations of a huge amount of material. But, unfortunately, they do not provide an integration of findings, give an explanation of negotiating processes or models for practical application. They do contain summaries of research material, which is of particular interest to scientists who want to form a picture of this field of research quickly.

DEVELOPMENT OF BROAD THEORIES

Several interesting studies have been undertaken in this field. For a while, a great deal was expected of game theory: a mathematical approach to negotiating processes. Game theory not only produced elegant models, but the ease with which it inspired empirical research made it look promising. An astute work in this field is:

- Bartos, O. J., *Process and Outcomes of Negotiations* (New York, Columbia University Press, 1974).

Surveys are given by:

Harsanyi, J. C., *Rational Behavior and Bargaining Equilibrium in Games and Social Situations* (New York, Cambridge University Press, 1977).

Rapoport, A., *Two-Person Game Theory* (Ann Arbor, University of Michigan Press, 1966).

Young, P. R. (ed.), *Bargaining: Formal Theories of Negotiation* (Chicago, University of Illinois Press, 1975).

Interest in the game theory approach seems to be waning. Its most important drawbacks are its high level of abstraction and its limited practicality.

There are also more descriptive and qualitative models of negotiations. They generally work along two lines: reports of concrete negotiation experiences in the form of observations or interviews on the one hand, and a coordinating and structuring framework on the other. In my view, this is among the more successful approaches, and, in many variations, it has found its way into publications with practical inclinations. The following is a standard work.

• Walton, R. E. and McKersie, R. B., *A Behavioral Theory of Labor Negotiations* (New York, McGraw Hill, 1965).

This classic deserves special mention. I reckon it is the most frequently quoted work on negotiating. Although the model it sketches has not really acquired a following, a few important aspects of it have gained wide popularity; for example, the distinction between distributive and integrative negotiating. My own work incorporates the idea of these authors that negotiating consists of several types of activities.

A type of descriptive model which has been worked on for some twenty-five years is the phase model of the negotiating process. On the basis of case studies, interviews, observations and personal experiences, an important literature has emerged in this field. The following works give a good impression of its range:

Albeda, W., *Arbeidsverhoudingen in Nederland* (chapter 3) (Alphen, Samsom, 1975).

Brock, J., *Bargaining beyond Impasse* (Boston, Auburn House, 1982).

Douglas, A., *Industrial Peacemaking* (New York, Columbia University Press, 1962).

Gullivers, P. H., *Disputes and Negotiations* (New York, Academic Press, 1979).

Himmelmann, G., *Lohnbildungen durch Kollektivverhandlungen* (Berlin, Duncker & Humboldt, 1971).

Zartman, W. and Berman, M. R., *The Practical Negotiator* (New Haven, Conn., Yale University Press, 1982).

The title of the last work shows that attempts are being made to turn to a practical elaboration of these models. Brock's book goes so far as to recommend working in phases, with outside interventions at certain points, to make the chance of failure as small as possible.

Interestingly enough, such studies mainly discuss very mature negotiating processes, for instance, in the field of diplomacy or in the relationship between employers and employees. It is my feeling that, with some adaptations, the results are quite useful to other types of negotiations. I have therefore tried to integrate their most important findings in my own work.

A few more recent books that attempt, each in its own way, to formulate more comprehensive theories are:

- Bacharach, S. B. and Lawler, E. J., *Bargaining: Power Tactics and Outcomes* (San Francisco, Jossey Bass, 1981).

The attractiveness but also the limitation of this book is that it focuses exclusively on one very essential aspect of negotiating: mutual dependency relations.

- Druckman, D. (ed.), *Negotiations: Social-Psychological Perspectives* (London, Sage, 1977).

An attempt to combine a large number of different perspectives.

- Pruitt, D. G., *Negotiation Behaviour* (London, Academic Press, 1981).

This book describes what it terms a 'general theory of negotiating'. Pruitt is more successful that Druckman in linking different models and approaches.

- Raiffa, H., *The Art and Science of Negotiation* (Cambridge, Mass., Harvard University Press, 1982).

A comprehensive work: theoretical insights, case studies, tactical and strategic tips and mathematical models.

- Strauss, A., *Negotiations: Varieties, Contexts, Processes and Social Order* (San Francisco, Calif., Jossey Bass, 1978).

This book elaborates what could better be called a 'philosophy' rather than a theory of negotiating.

- Dupont, C., *La négociation: Conduite, théorie, applications* (Paris, Dalloz, 1982).

This is a survey of both the most important theories and many practical strategies and tactics. While not a long book, it is highly comprehensive. What makes it especially interesting is that, in addition to the Anglo-Saxon literature, it also treats French authors, who are usually unfamiliar to us.

Two other books, interesting because they contribute to our knowledge of *negotiating inside organizations*, are:

- Lax, D. A. and Sebenius, J. K., *The Manager as Negotiator* (New York, Free Press, 1986).
- Bazerman, M. H. and Lewicki, R. J. (eds), *Negotiating in Organizations* (Beverly Hills, Calif., Sage, 1983).

For those who want to keep up with the latest developments, there is: *Negotiation Journal*, 'On the Process of Dispute Settlement', Plenum Publishing Corporation, 233 Spring Street, New York, NY 10013.

APPENDIX 2

Training in Negotiating

How can we teach negotiating? Reading this book and among the works cited in Appendix 1 is one way; but reading must be supplemented by experience. This appendix sets out various practical exercises, beginning with simple questionnaires and moving on to more complex simulations. These exercises, together with the evaluation forms and summaries which follow, provide ample practical material for a training workshop, and a suggested programme for a two-day seminar of this kind is presented at the end of the appendix.

The tables and figures that appear throughout the book also summarize significant aspects of negotiation and should be used in conjunction with the material in this appendix.

Questionnaire 1 'What is negotiating?'

Which of the statements below do you think should
characterize negotiating, which do not fit?

1 One emphasizes one's goals as superior   YES/NO

2 One makes occasional attempts to tip the power balance in
   one's favour   YES/NO

3 Personal problems are openly discussed for mutual support
   to each other   YES/NO

4 Threats and confusion are used moderately and
   measured   YES/NO

5 One presents one's interests accurately   YES/NO

6 One's attitude is concentrated on 'what can *I* get out
   of this   YES/NO

7 One is one-sided in the facts one presents   YES/NO

8 Every opportunity is used to dominate   YES/NO

Questionnaire 2 'What is negotiating?'

Which of the statements below do you think should
characterize negotiating, which do not fit?

1 In negotiating it is essential to win   YES/NO

2 A good tactic in negotiation is to keep the opposite party
   divided and opposed to each other   YES/NO

3 A good negotiating tactic is to bring the negotiations to an
   impasse   YES/NO

4 In negotiating, you must present all the information at
   your disposal   YES/NO

5 You must never exploit the personal sensitivity of your
   opponent   YES/NO

6 Treat your opponent as an equal as long as this produces
   success   YES/NO

7 Never show emotions and irritations   YES/NO

8 Don't hesitate to emphasize facts favourable to your
   position   YES/NO

9 Never do something to your opponent that you would not
   do to a good friend   YES/NO

10 Try to develop a good relationship with your
    opponent   YES/NO

11 It is often wise not to wring the maximum concessions
    from your opponent   YES/NO

12 It is better to do business with an opponent who has much
    experience than with a novice   YES/NO

Mini-exercise 1 Edelweiss

At the ski station Edelweiss, a day ticket costs £18 and a half-day ticket £12. A skier who bought a day ticket in the morning discovers at noon that, for a reason he did not foresee, he can no longer ski.

By chance he meets a person who is about to buy a half-day ticket; he proposes to this person that he sell him his day ticket.

What will the price of the transaction be?

Mini-exercise 2 Arrive at a favourable result while maintaining a good relationship

Goal This exercise is particularly useful for clarifying the 'exploring-avoiding' dimension. (Earlier versions of this exercise were developed for research purposes; see Pruitt and Lewis, 1975; Shulz and Pruitt, 1978.)

Set-up Participants are divided into sellers and buyers. Everybody receives the general information and their own – but only their own – list of profits. Each group takes a few minutes to prepare for the negotiation. The actual negotiating takes place on a one-to-one basis, with everybody operating as one of a pair.

Duration Around 15 minutes.

GENERAL INFORMATION

A buyer negotiates with a seller. The buyer represents a large shop; the seller represents a factory. The two have a long-standing relationship of doing business with each other. Prices are expressed by the letters A to I. A deal has been made if there is an agreement on a letter for each product.

It is important to keep in mind that except for the three prices (to be expressed by three letters), everything else relating to the sale has already been decided upon: specifications, amounts, models, colours, delivery schedules, etc. have all been fixed in earlier meetings. Do not show your list of prices and profits.

LIST OF PRICES AND PROFITS FOR THE BUYER

Television sets		Compact disc players		Video sets	
Price	Profit	Price	Profit	Price	Profit
A	£200	A	£120	A	£80
B	£175	B	£105	B	£70
C	£150	C	£ 90	C	£60
D	£125	D	£ 75	D	£50
E	£100	E	£ 60	E	£40
F	£ 75	F	£ 45	F	£30
G	£ 50	G	£ 30	G	£20
H	£ 25	H	£ 15	H	£10
I	£ 00	I	£ 00	I	£00

LIST OF PRICES AND PROFITS FOR THE SELLER

Television sets		Compact disc players		Video sets	
Price	Profit	Price	Profit	Price	Profit
A	£00	A	£ 00	A	£ 00
B	£10	B	£ 15	B	£ 25
C	£20	C	£ 30	C	£ 50
D	£30	D	£ 45	D	£ 75
E	£40	E	£ 60	E	£100
F	£50	F	£ 75	F	£125
G	£60	G	£ 90	G	£150
H	£70	H	£105	H	£175
I	£80	I	£120	I	£200

Mini-exercise 3 Shark Island

On one of their joint adventures the three famous bandits, Popof, Totor and Bébert, learn of the existence of a treasure worth £1,000,000 in gold and silver, which is buried on Shark Island. The three pirates are skilled negotiators, and in a corner of the tavern they discuss the division of the treasure. An essential element of the discussion is that Popof and Totor each have a boat while Bébert does not. But because of the constantly dangerous weather conditions around the island, it is absolutely imperative that at least two people be in one boat. An additional factor complicates the matter: Totor's boat is rather dilapidated. Even in the best circumstances he could only make the trip once and only take along half of the treasure.

All three would like to preserve the existing mutual ties in order to pursue future joint adventures.

What sort of agreement do the three arrive at?

Mini-exercise 4 Accumulate as many points as possible

This is a variant of the 'prisoner's dilemma' game, probably the most frequently used conflict management and negotiation exercise. The exercise is so simple that, at first, the participants hardly understand it. But this only lasts for one or two transactions.

Goal To demonstrate how easily parties can allow themselves to be drawn into strong rivalries, thus preventing them from making good use of mutual dependency and integrative potential.

Set-up Four groups of three to four persons, divided among the four corners of a room, each group to constitute one 'department'.

Start Each participant is given forms 1 and 2. They get about five minutes to prepare themselves for the first transaction. If necessary, the game leader explains the scoring system. He indicates when each transaction may begin, and writes down the outcome of each transaction, or the choices of the various departments, on the board.

Duration 35 minutes.

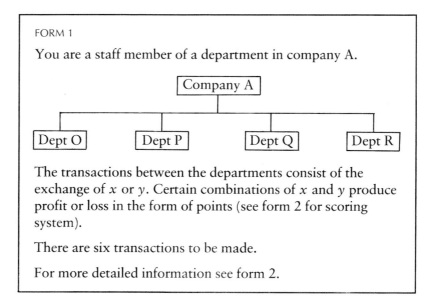

FORM 1

You are a staff member of a department in company A.

Company A

Dept O   Dept P   Dept Q   Dept R

The transactions between the departments consist of the exchange of x or y. Certain combinations of x and y produce profit or loss in the form of points (see form 2 for scoring system).

There are six transactions to be made.

For more detailed information see form 2.

FORM 2

Scoring chart

Trans-action	Choice	Profit points	Loss points	Balance
1				
2				
3				
4				
5				
6				

Scoring system

4 Xs	Loss	1 point
3 Xs	Profit	1 point
1 Y	Loss	3 points
2 Xs	Profit	2 points
2 Ys	Loss	2 points
1 X	Profit	3 points
3 Ys	Loss	1 point
4 Ys	Profit	1 point

- There are 6 transactions.
- A transaction consists of the input of x or y by each of the four departments.
- The result of each transaction is a certain combination of xs and ys. From the scoring system you can determine how many points you win or lose.
- In the third and fifth transactions consultation with other departments is required. Each department should therefore delegate one person for this purpose.
- You can keep track of your total of points by means of the scoring formula.
- Your profit or loss in rounds 3, 5 and 6 is to be multiplied by 3, 5 and 10 respectively.

Simulation 1 The Real Estate exercise

Goal This exercise can be a good demonstration of the various dilemmas and types of activities that are important in negotiating. If the delegations score one another on evaluation forms (see p. 157), the group can look afterwards at how the parties were able to cope with the various dilemmas.

Set-up Four delegations of one to three persons.

Start Each participant receives his role instructions and a map of the site. About 10–15 minutes of preparation time is allowed.

Duration Around 45 minutes.

The 'real estate' exercise: map of site

A1 UK	A2 University	A3 Fairway	A4 University
B1 University	B2 London Investment	B3 Fairway	B4 Fairway
C1 London Investment	C2 Fairway	C3 London Investment	C4 UK
D1 UK	D2 UK	D3 London Investment	D4 UK

N

W ——|—— E

S

LONDON INVESTMENT TRUST LTD

You are a member of London Investment Trust Ltd. Your company is the owner of plots B2, C1, C3 and D3.

Your company would like to obtain plots B2, B3 and C2, C3; or C2, C3 and D2, D3. These plots will be used for the construction of a shopping centre. All your actual preferences are based on a square plot of land with department stores in the middle and with plenty of parking space around it. Some of your contacts have informed you that a highway is projected in the area; you do not know exactly where.

Funds available for this investment: £1,000,000.

Plots are normally sold at £500,000 each.

Other companies involved:
- UK Construction Ltd
- Fairway Construction Ltd
- University Construction Office

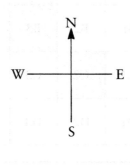

A1	A2	A3	A4
B1	B2	B3	B4
C1	C2	C3	C4
D1	D2	D3	D4

FAIRWAY CONSTRUCTION LTD

You are a member of Fairway Construction Ltd. Your company owns plots A3, B3, B4 and C2.

Your company hopes to acquire the plots A4, B4, C4 and D4, because a strip in the middle of these plots has been earmarked for a new highway. This will make the land on both sides of the projected highway very expensive. The news about the highway is not officially known. If it is published it is probable that prices of plots will go up. The plots are at present normally sold for £500,000 each.

Funds available for this investment: $1,000,000.

Other companies involved:
- UK Construction Ltd
- University Construction Office
- London Investment Trust Ltd

A1	A2	A3	A4
B1	B2	B3	B4
C1	C2	C3	C4
D1	D2	D3	D4

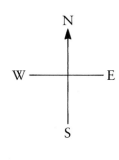

UK CONSTRUCTION LTD

You are a member of UK Construction Ltd. At present, your company owns plots A1, C4, D1, D2 and D4.

Your company wants to obtain four plots which link up in a long stretched rectangle in order to develop a modern housing project. Your company does not have at its disposal all the necessary financial means for the construction of the houses. Therefore it aims to obtain more money by selling one of the five plots it already owns. If a rectangle of four proves impossible to obtain, reconsider an L-shape of the plots; it will be costly to adapt the original plan, and it will not be easy to convince your superiors.

Plots are normally sold at £500,000 each, but you might be able to make more than this.

Other companies involved:
- Fairway Construction Ltd
- University Construction Office
- London Investment Trust Ltd

A1	A2	A3	A4
B1	B2	B3	B4
C1	C2	C3	C4
D1	D2	D3	D4

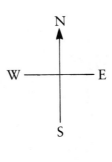

UNIVERSITY CONSTRUCTION OFFICE

You are a member of the University Construction Office. With future development plans in view, the office acquired plots A2, A4 and B1 some time ago.

Since policy is focusing more and more on concentration of university buildings, you hope to arrive at a group of three blocks which link up in a rectangle by buying and selling the three separate plots.

Since you do not have a separate budget for this transaction, you must create some financial leeway for yourself by negotiating a profitable outcome.

If you cannot manage to obtain the plots in a rectangle, the construction plans could be adapted to an L-shape. It would take quite some energy, time and money to change the original plans.

Plots are normally sold at £500,000 each but this price will go up if two groups are trying to outbid each other or if some development is raising the attractiveness of the plot concerned. In this context, you happen to know of existing plans for a highway and a big shopping centre.

Other companies involved:
- London Investment Trust Ltd
- UK Construction Ltd
- Fairway Construction Ltd

A1	A2	A3	A4
B1	B2	B3	B4
C1	C2	C3	C4
D1	D2	D3	D4

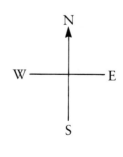

Simulation 2 The London Company exercise

Goals This exercise has two goals:

- the practice of chairmanship
- the pratice of negotiating styles

Set-up Five individuals who will all participate in the same meeting.

Start Each participant receives the general information, the organizational chart and his role instructions. 15 minutes preparation time is allowed.

GENERAL INFORMATION

The London Company produces metal components. During the past 15 years the company has developed in a dynamic way. The present general manager was recruited 16 years ago as head of research and development, which had until then been a neglected department. Together with some new colleagues, he made a number of patented inventions. During that period, the company grew into a medium-sized firm with a positive image in its markets. Nine years after joining the firm he was appointed general manager of the London Company.

After a period of stagnation, this year the order backlog has increased considerably (8% net).

Up to now, additions to personnel have always been directly negotiated by departmental heads with the general manager and deputy general manager. These negotiations normally started when a need for more staff became obvious. The absence of a stricter system has led to friction and jealousy, because people could easily get the impression that others were unjustifiably privileged, and that they were being played off against each other.

After much perseverance with the idea, the deputy general manager now has proposed a trial of a different system, which is:

- an inventory of personnel requirements by all three departmental heads, followed by

- a plenary meeting in which the various claims will be discussed in terms of feasibility.

The general manager is not in favour of this trial and has stated clearly that if the new procedure fails, the old system will be re-introduced. If that happens, the people involved will have to accept its well-known disadvantages; it will also imply that recruitment efforts will be delayed. The old system also means that there will be a minimum allocation of ±2 employees at any one time.

The total number of additional staff places available at this moment is 16.

The meeting starts now; you have 50 minutes to come to a distribution of these vacancies.

Organization chart

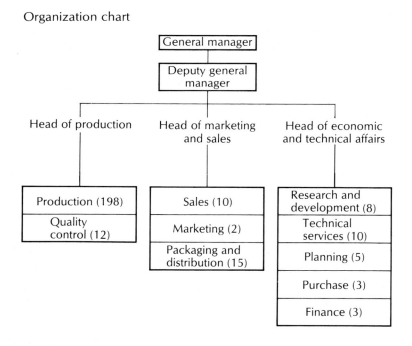

DEPUTY GENERAL MANAGER

The discussion about the distribution of new employees will start after you have received a written request from all three departmental heads.

You will start the meeting by announcing the three requests and by stating that the recruitment of new employees will be limited to 16.

You do not have a personal interest in the final distribution, but of course the outcome must convince you that it serves the interests of the company.

You also think it is very important that the relationship between the three departmental heads should not be influenced negatively.

HEAD OF PRODUCTION

In the first place you have to deliver your request for additional personnel in your department to the deputy general manager. It concerns only the total amount.

In relation to your request and the discussion which will take place, the following arguments will be essential:

- For this year alone, an 8% production increase is necessary. Only 2%–4% could be achieved by technical adaptations.
- The increase will be mainly in the plastic components production line. Until now you have reached your targets by transferring personnel for a limited period from other production lines to the plastic components line. You are fed up with this improvisation, particularly because the working climate in production is affected by it.
- Your department is the backbone of the company. It is your department that earns the money. The other departments are only supportive. National and local papers publish articles pointing out that 'indirect' workers in other companies are being fired. In your company, people would be happy if the present employment level in the support departments could be maintained.

HEAD OF MARKETING AND SALES

In the first place you have to deliver your request for additional personnel in your department to the deputy general manager. It concerns only the total amount.

In relation to your request and the discussion which will take place, the following arguments will be essential:

- Your marketing department hasn't got much impact in this company. If this discipline is to have a serious opportunity to have some impact in the organization, high-quality marketing experts will have to be recruited as soon as possible.
- Marketing is becoming more and more important; the time is past when this company was able to survive by means of some incidental and intuitive ideas from management. Medium- and long-range market opportunities must be examined; this is of crucial importance if the company wants to ensure its survival and development.
- The company was enabled to survive through the recent recession period by the tremendous efforts of the sales people. Competition is becoming more and more severe. Frequent and personal contacts between sales and customers is becoming a primary condition for being successful in this market.
- Industrial fairs, too, are becoming more and more important. Until recently, this only involved a few events at a national level. Today there is a tendency to organize fairs at a local and regional level.
- As a result of the stress caused by the increased efforts required from a limited sales force, you are confronted with a striking increase in employee turnover (6%) and absenteeism (15%).

HEAD OF ECONOMIC AND TECHNICAL AFFAIRS

In the first place you have to deliver your request for additional personnel in your department to the deputy general manager. It concerns only the total amount.

In relation to your request and the discussion which will take place, the following arguments will be essential:

- Research and development have made the company what it is now. Growth in the various groups of products has been stimulated primarily by research and development. At this point it is obvious that plastic components, developed by your department, is potentially the strongest line in the company.
- Besides innovation in the plastic component area, your policy will also be to direct more attention towards finding creative solutions with regard to already existing products. In fact, your department has quite a record as far as innovation is concerned.
- You know that the general manager has a weak spot for research and development. You are sure that you could easily get his approval for the recruitment of *two employees*.
- Increasing absenteeism (a 3% increase during the last two years) should be compensated for by new people.
- The load on the maintenance department is going to be heavily increased by the growth of the new plastic components production line. In addition, adaptations to existing product lines demand more and more attention. It is company policy to achieve an increase in production volume through adaptations of production methods.
- The maintenance department will have more activities as a consequence of the increase in research and development efforts. For example, it is frequently involved in the execution of experimental constructions.

Simulation 3 The pollution of the Rhine: a simulation of international negotiations

The four delegations have agreed that the negotiations will begin 50 minutes from now, having already received the General Preliminary Information and information on their own countries.

You may use this time for preparation. Try especially to formulate your interests in regard to content and your strategy. Preliminary contacts with other delegations are possible if so wished.

You have two hours for the negotiations themselves. You may adjourn as often as you like during this period. After 45 minutes there is a mandatory adjournment of the deliberations.

Your final product will be a joint text for a treaty concerning the pollution of the Rhine.

Note: It is not intended that you get bogged down in technical discussions. Points 5 and 6 of the agenda should in any case be dealt with.

GENERAL PRELIMINARY INFORMATION

All participants in the negotiations are officials who work directly under the responsible ministers. The ministers are agreed that a treaty must be concluded in the very near future. Their assignment is to negotiate an agreement regarding the protection of the Rhine from chemical pollution.

The negotiations have been prepared by an international commission of officials and scientists, hereafter referred to as the International Commission. The participating countries are Switzerland, Germany, France and the Netherlands.

The Netherlands place a high priority on concluding a Rhine agreement. The negotiations are important for Germany, which needs a large amount of Rhine water for drinking purposes for the Ruhr area, but is, however, by far the main polluter. France has so far shown little interest in the treaty. Switzerland will cooperate but does not accord the agreement a high priority. All countries have an interest in some tangible agreement.

In preparatory meetings the following agenda has been agreed upon:

1 Draw up a list of substances for which a dumping prohibition will apply.
2 Draw up a list of substances which may be dumped up to an agreed maximum limit.
3 Settle the specific maxima for the substances under 2.
4 Arrive at a formula for dividing the maxima among the countries.
5 Agree on a monitoring system.
6 Agree on the implementation of the agreement.

It was further agreed that the chairmanship will rotate among the delegations. France will supply the chairman for the first conference period.

On points 1, 2 and 3 of agenda

The following is an extract from a report by the International Commission.
'The following list indicates those substances which pollute the water of the Rhine in such a way that they may be considered to be of danger for the following purposes:

1 The preparation of drinking water for human consumption.
2 The direct or indirect supply of sweet water to the land for agricultural purposes.
3 The maintenance of an acceptable quality of the sea water.
4 The preservation and maintenance of the natural flora and fauna, as well as the maintenance of the ability of the water to purify itself and thereby of related goals such as fishing and recreation.

The substances are listed in a specific sequence. Those at the top of the list are the most destructive for the above purposes while the substances towards the bottom of the list can be tolerated as long as they do not exceed a given limit.

The commission itself was not able to agree on an unambiguous conclusion as to which substances should be absolutely forbidden. They were only able to agree that the first three substances should be prohibited.

The commission was also unable to agree on the tolerable limits. For each substance both the lowest and highest limit suggested in the commission by the various delegates is indicated in units of weight per m^3. The present level of dumping is also given.'

List of harmful substances prepared by the International Commission

	Lowest limit	Highest limit	Present level
1 Halogen compounds	0	0	2
2 Mercury and mercury compounds	0	0	3
3 Compounds of which it is demonstrated that they can cause cancer in or through the water	0	0	1
4 Persistent mineral oils and persistent hydrocarbons made from petroleum	0	18	22
5 Cyanides	0	8	12
6 Tin and tin compounds	0	8	6
7 Cadmium and cadmium compounds	4	12	11
8 Inorganic phosphorus compounds and elementary phosphorus	8	18	24
9 Lead and lead compounds	5	7	18
10 Chromium and chromium compounds	9	11	13
11 Ammonia and nitrites	3	5	10
12 Organic silicon compounds which are toxic and persistent	7	9	8

On point 4 of agenda

Three alternative criteria are given by the commission for dividing the permitted dumping maxima among the different countries.

1 Population.
2 Length of river banks of Rhine in that country.
3 A ratio proportional to the amount dumped by each country.

On point 5 of agenda

Two proposals were made to monitor the implementation and observance of the treaty.

1 French proposal: leave it up to the individual country.
2 Dutch proposal: enlarge the international commission and assign them the following tasks:

a draw up and maintain lists of all the main dumpers (cities and companies);

b for every dumping of the agreed substances require a permit with a limited duration in which the permitted emission is specified;

c permanent measuring network (every 150 km) that makes measurements continually;

d mobile measuring units to make sample tests elsewhere to localize precisely the polluters;

e make agreements with the local authorities in order to be able to take the necessary steps, including such sanctions as penal prosecution, in the case of violations.

On point 6 of agenda

French proposal: As soon as the treaty has been ratified by each parliament, each country will proceed to implement the agreements. Once every three years the International Commission will meet to exchange data about the degree of implementation achieved.

Dutch proposal: Insert a clause in the treaty requiring each country to draw up and implement a national programme such that their own part of the agreement will be effected within three years after the treaty has been ratified by their parliaments.

German proposal: As the French proposal, but International Commission to meet once every two years; also, countries to be required to implement agreements within five years.

SWITZERLAND

The negotiations do not have a high priority for you. You are not bothered by what other countries dump in the Rhine. With regard to total amounts you are not the largest polluter of the four; furthermore, about half of the Rhine water ultimately comes from Switzerland.

Yet there are people in your country, especially in the tourist sector, who are urging that measures should be taken. Some of the lakes are becoming rather polluted. Up to now companies and cities have been subject to few restrictions as to dumping. Your delegation agrees that something should happen, but the financial costs for the industrial sector and for the various governments should be taken into account.

Your national politics have always been concerned with maintaining good relations with France and Germany. Your own delegation is predominantly French Swiss. In the future you yourself will have to deal primarily with the French. This will of course play a role but not so as to interfere with the national political concerns mentioned above.

Finally, it is the policy of your country to be very cautious in accepting international inspections and never to enter into troublesome commitments. National autonomy is crucial in Swiss foreign policy.

FRANCE

Your direct interests in a Rhine chemical treaty are minimal. You need very little Rhine water for drinking and irrigation purposes, and chemical pollution by French industry is still small, although national industrialization makes increased pollution likely. Your industries are at present in a relatively difficult position as a result of international competition. Environmental legislation that is rigorous and costly for the industrial sector is therefore not in your interest.

You would like to make the dumping restrictions as flexible as possible and, where this does not succeed, to delay when you can. At the same time you realize that you must exercise necessary caution with this policy because otherwise you will antagonize the Germans and especially the Dutch. If relations deteriorate too much, this could make other talks and agreements with these countries more difficult, and this is also not desirable. These relations are already under pressure because of bickering about monetary adjustments.

You will supply the chairman for the first conference period.

THE NETHERLANDS

You are very interested in a Rhine treaty. Drinking water, water for agricultural uses, cleaner sea water, recreational and environmental concerns are important things for you. Not only are parliament and the government very concerned about these issues but so is public opinion. The negotiations will be followed very closely. Television and the press have used this occasion to devote extensive reports to the importance and the present condition of the Rhine water.

After the extensive preparations undertaken by the international commission you are counting on tangible results. This should be possible. But the other countries are less interested in reaching a solution.

Because the responsible ministers have decided that an agreement must be made, and since no one wants deteriorated relations to deteriorate, and because agreements have been made and talks are continuing in many other areas, you expect a sympathetic attitude on the part of the other delegations.

Some opposition, however, is expected from the French, who do not want their national prerogatives to be infringed upon. Furthermore, they need the Rhine for drinking, recreational and agricultural purposes much less than do Germany and the Netherlands. On the other hand, the French need to put some effort into relations with their European partners, having recently placed these relations under some strain in connection with, for example, monetary adjustments.

You are counting on some understanding of the fact that the Netherlands is the greatest victim of Rhine pollution. Your general starting point on financial questions is: the pollutant pays.

GERMANY

These negotiations are very important for you. Besides a certain 'sentimental' interest in a clean Rhine (respecting tourism and recreation), a great deal of Rhine water is used for drinking purposes. Your very extensive chemical industries on the Rhine play a vital part in the German economy and also have great political influence. If the costs for the industrial sector due to environmental measures (including possible measures against air pollution) are too high, some companies may transfer to other countries. That would be unacceptable economically, as well as in employment terms. But on the other hand you must consider the recent rise of the Green Party. Your government would like to take the wind out of the Greens' sails by chalking up a success in the environmental sphere.

You are aware that France is not very interested in the negotiations. Some opposition is expected from them, for they do not want their national prerogatives to be infringed upon. Furthermore, they need the Rhine for drinking, recreational and agricultural purposes much less than Germany and the Netherlands. On the other hand, the French need to put some effort into relations with their European partners, having recently placed these relations under some strain in connection with monetary adjustments, for example. You want to work towards concrete agreements, although relations between the negotiating partners should not thereby be harmed.

You can understand that the Dutch are most eager for a treaty. All the waste flows through their delta, and then resurfaces on their coast. It is not surprising that Dutch public opinion and environmental groups are so concerned about the environment. In your own country the issue takes a less high priority with public opinion and the parliament (with the exception of the Greens, of course).

Evaluation Form 1 Negotiating behaviour: fighting, cooperation, flexibility

Characterize the behaviour of the negotiators by giving it a score of 1 to 5 on each of the following two lines:

1 How does the negotiator maintain the tension between 'cooperation' and 'fighting'?

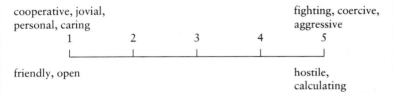

cooperative, jovial,   fighting, coercive,
personal, caring   aggressive

        1   2   3   4   5

friendly, open   hostile,
                                                        calculating

2 How flexible in his strategy is the negotiator?

        1   2   3   4   5

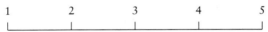

flexible, active,   avoiding, staying on
seeking background   one track, rigid,
information, open to   repetitive, passive,
alternatives, exploring,   detached, evasive
improvising, alert

Note: It is possible for one to be avoiding in a very active way. For example, by repeating the same arguments in different forms while sticking to one's original premises, defending a certain solution at all costs or making the issue a question of principle.

Suggestions

Evaluation form 2 Negotiating behaviour: flexibility, personal relations, power

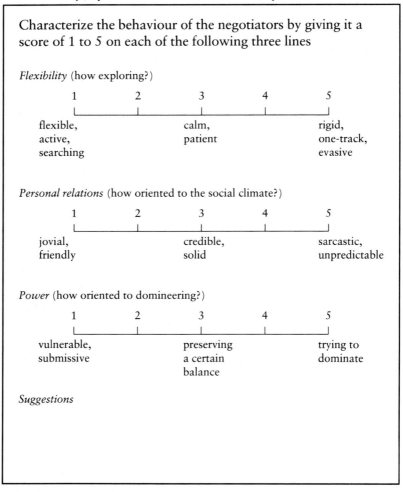

Characterize the behaviour of the negotiators by giving it a score of 1 to 5 on each of the following three lines

Flexibility (how exploring?)

1	2	3	4	5

flexible,   calm,   rigid,
active,   patient   one-track,
searching   evasive

Personal relations (how oriented to the social climate?)

1	2	3	4	5

jovial,   credible,   sarcastic,
friendly   solid   unpredictable

Power (how oriented to domineering?)

1	2	3	4	5

vulnerable,   preserving   trying to
submissive   a certain   dominate
                     balance

Suggestions

Evaluation form 3 Your negotiating profile

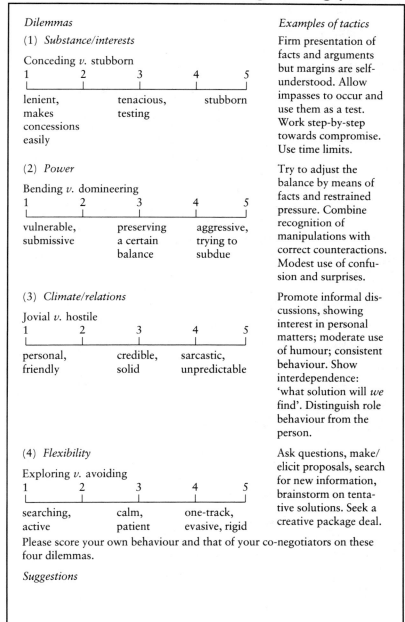

Dilemmas

(1) *Substance/interests*

Conceding *v.* stubborn

1	2	3	4	5

lenient, makes concessions easily

tenacious, testing

stubborn

(2) *Power*

Bending *v.* domineering

1	2	3	4	5

vulnerable, submissive

preserving a certain balance

aggressive, trying to subdue

(3) *Climate/relations*

Jovial *v.* hostile

1	2	3	4	5

personal, friendly

credible, solid

sarcastic, unpredictable

(4) *Flexibility*

Exploring *v.* avoiding

1	2	3	4	5

searching, active

calm, patient

one-track, evasive, rigid

Please score your own behaviour and that of your co-negotiators on these four dilemmas.

Suggestions

Examples of tactics

Firm presentation of facts and arguments but margins are self-understood. Allow impasses to occur and use them as a test. Work step-by-step towards compromise. Use time limits.

Try to adjust the balance by means of facts and restrained pressure. Combine recognition of manipulations with correct counteractions. Modest use of confusion and surprises.

Promote informal discussions, showing interest in personal matters; moderate use of humour; consistent behaviour. Show interdependence: 'what solution will *we* find'. Distinguish role behaviour from the person.

Ask questions, make/elicit proposals, search for new information, brainstorm on tentative solutions. Seek a creative package deal.

Summary 1 Personal negotiating styles

Four basic negotiating styles may be identified:

1 *The ethical style*, characterized by trust and belief in common interests, principles and values, setting high standards, developing proposals in the common interest, independent thinking, sticking to principles.
2 *The analytical–aggressive style*, characterized by careful analysis, preference for hard facts and figures, sound logic, weighing all alternatives ahead of time, reliance on sound procedures, keeping things predictable, holding firmly on to goals.
3 *The jovial style*, characterized by good social skills, personal charm, being diplomatic, influencing the climate positively, eagerness to try things out, sensitivity to integrative solutions, flexibility.
4 *The flexible–aggressive style*, characterized by desire to get things done, liking for accomplishment, taking advantage of opportunities, keeping things on the move, liking challenges.

Is one of the four styles dominant? Which of the four is most strongly represented in your behaviour? Each style also has its less effective side. Learn to recognize the less effective aspects of your style.

1 The ethical style
Less productive aspects when used in excess: becomes 'preachy', withdraws and is not open to new ideas, is too concerned with ideals and common values to the point of being unrealistic.
Tendencies in a conflict: sticks to his case because he is right or gives in, disappointed. Becomes disillusioned, is set apart.

2 The analytical–aggressive style
Less productive aspects when used in excess: sticks to the same track, too little sensitivity to the climate of the discussions, over-preoccupation with details, no ability to improvise.
Tendencies in a conflict: amasses more and more 'evidence' that he is right, becomes stubborn.

3 The jovial style
Less productive aspects when used in excess: avoids a test of strength, offers too little resistance, becomes ambivalent.

Tendencies in a conflict: overcompromising, gives in to preserve harmony and good will.

4 **The flexible–aggressive style**
   Less productive aspects when used in excess: bossy, gives others too few chances, easily becomes impatient and impulsive.
   Tendencies in a conflict: does not concede, even when he knows he is wrong, becomes angry, tends to coercive pressure, tries everything within his power to win his case.

Mark the elements in your style (or styles) that sometimes characterize your behaviour.

The four styles are mixtures of two basic dimensions of negotiating, thus:

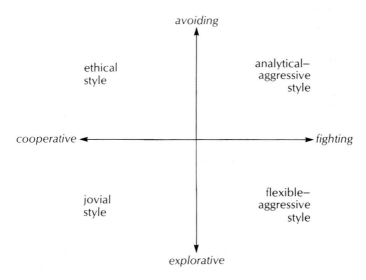

Place yourself in this quadrant on the basis of the information that you have obtained about your behaviour during the exercises. Compare this with previous assessments of your own style during the exercises. Finally, with one or two other participants, compare your assessments and also try to score one another's negotiating styles in the quadrant.

Summary 2 Cooperation, negotiation, fighting

- *Cooperation* is appropriate if interests and goals are similar. It is the obvious method if the benefits for those concerned are directly dependent on the degree to which they can pool their resources.
- *Negotiation* is the correct strategy when interests are different or opposed if there is so much mutual dependence that an agreement has advantages for both parties. In this case, parties disagree but are willing to come to an agreement because letting things drift or fighting would be disadvantageous for both parties.
- *Fighting* is the most likely strategy when either party thinks it can win more by fighting than by negotiating. Sometimes it is used from a powerless position to build up a strong negotiating position. A fighting strategy is concerned with obtaining mastery. One tries to reduce the opponent to submission.

Features of cooperation, negotiating and fighting

Cooperation	Negotiation	Fighting
Conflict is seen as a common problem.	Conflict is seen as a clash between different but mutually dependent interests.	Conflict is seen as a question of 'winning or losing'.
People present their own goals as accurately as possible.	People exaggerate their own interests but pay attention to possible areas of agreement.	People emphasize the superiority of their own objectives.
Each other's weak points and personal problems can be openly discussed.	Personal problems are disguised or very circumspectly presented.	Personal problems do not exist.
The information provided is honest.	The information given is one-sided. The facts favourable to one's own party are deliberately emphasized.	If it can help to make the opponent submit, false information is deliberately spread.

Cooperation	Negotiation	Fighting
Discussion subjects are presented in terms of underlying problems.	Agenda are formulated in terms of alternative solutions.	Points of disagreement are formulated in terms of one's own solution.
Possible solutions are tested against their practical consequences and common criteria.	Occasionally the linking of solutions to principles is used to put some pressure on the other side.	One's own solutions are rigidly tied to higher principles.
Speaking out for one particular solution is deliberately delayed as long as possible.	A preference for a particular solution is shown, but a scope for concessions is self-evident.	An absolute and unconditioinal preference for one's own solution is expressed at every opportunity.
Threatening, creating confusion, and taking advantage of the mistakes of others are seen as detrimental.	Occasionally a modest and carefully calculated use is made of threats, confusion and surprise.	Threats, confusion, shock effects, etc., are welcome at any time to reduce the opponent to submission.
Active participation of all concerned is encouraged.	Contacts between parties are limited to a few spokesmen.	Contacts between the parties take place indirectly via statements.
An attempt is made to spread power as much as possible and to let it play no further role.	Occasionally each other's power is tested, or attempts are made to influence the balance of power in one's own favour.	Both parties are engaged in a permanent power struggle.
People try to understand each other and share each other's personal concerns.	Understanding the views of the other side is seen as a tactical instrument.	No one bothers to understand the opponent.
Personal irritations are expressed to clear the air of tensions that could hamper future cooperation.	Personal irritations are suppressed or ventilated indirectly (e.g., with humour).	Irritations confirm negative and hostile images. Hostility is expressed to break down the other side.
Both parties find it easy to call in outside expertise to help in decision-making.	Third parties are brought in only if there is a complete deadlock.	Outsiders are welcome only if they are 'blind' supporters.

The borders between these three types of behaviour are not clear-cut. The three approaches can be visualized as existing on a continuum where one flows over into the next. It is sometimes striking how easily one allows oneself to be carried along into a *shift to the fighting strategy*. This behaviour is often triggered off by a reference to the *'less constructive behaviour' of the opponent*; but the opponent is having exactly the same experience, and thus the situation deteriorates.

This type of process, by which parties manoeuvre clumsily and so become entangled in conflicts and prestige disputes, often occurs spontaneously and without intention. Later the participants see to their embarrassment that they are caught in a mutually reinforcing spiral of hostilities. Insight into these 'spontaneous' forces and a broad repertoire of alternative behaviour can prevent unwanted shifts towards destructive conflicts. The two tables in this summary identify the range of behavioural tendencies and tactical approaches characteristic of the three strategies.

Examples of different use of tactics

	Cooperation	Negotiation	Fighting
Obtaining material results			
Goals and interests	presented accurately	exaggerated	emphasized as superior
Facts presented	complete	one-sided	false
Influencing the climate			
Personal problems	openly dis-cussed for mutual support	not taken advantage of	used to break down oppo-nent
General attitude	your interest is my interest	what deal will *we* make	what can *I* get out of this
Influencing the balance of power			
Power balance	horizontal, not questioned	occasional and calculated pulls	questioned at every oppor-tunity
Threats and confu-sion	seen as detri-mental	used moder-ately	used on any occasion

Summary 3 The chairman's role: a checklist

- State:
  - objectives;
  - conditions (time, consequences of no decision);
  - procedures.
- Create the opportunity for everyone to clarify his claims:
  - level of claims;
  - why this claim, arguments;
  - no discussion yet.
- Recapitulate; suggest alternative ways to find solutions.
- What do the different interests really imply, what are the consequences?

Transform information into integrative proposals.

- Stimulate parties to make integrative proposals.
- Increase pressure (time is up!, the consequence of no decision will be . . .! etc.)
- State a 'platform' proposal which
  - expresses the actual balance of power;
  - keeps all parties in the same boat;
  - gives some advantages to the parties who are using accepted criteria.
- Let parties amend and specify the 'platform' proposal.

HOW TO AVOID A FIGHTING SITUATION

1 By cutting off *personal* attacks.
2 By keeping the parties in balance. Never accept any party becoming the scapegoat or the only one to make sacrifices.
3 By being careful with discussions about principles; extensive arguments, references to higher values and norms may stimulate polarization.

Summary 4 Haves and have-nots

The table gives an overview of the dynamics of a situation pre-conditioned by

- a substantial difference in power between two parties but also
- a fairly strong interdependency.

	'Spontaneous' dynamics	Possible alternatives
'HAVES'	• Overestimation of own power: feelings of 'we are all right, no need to be really concerned.' • Underestimation of inter-dependence: feelings of 'we don't need them, they need us.' • Underestimation of integra-tive potential: 1 No searching for negoti-able areas. 'We can't do much.' 2 No openness or specific info about own limita-tions.	Notion of the dynamics to-ward escalation and some uneasiness about it. Diagnosis of own interests: • How bad are the con-sequences of an escalation for us? • How interdependent are we?
	Superior stand in meetings • Why don't you trust us. We'll handle the matter in a responsible way. • Ridicule, tough attitude. 'These people have to know their place.'	Explorative attitude in meet-ings • How do we establish an explorative climate? Loca-tion, agenda, behaviour. • What do they want? What are our interests and limita-tions?
	Tunnel vision: 'We want the best but these people are irresponsible, agressive, criminal, etc.' 'If they want to fight, they can have it. We can't help it.'	*Negotiations*.
	Escalation into fighting or into a deadlock with substantial losses for both parties.	The above mentioned strategy consists of two phases: 1 Diagnosis and exploration. 2 Negotiations.

	'Spontaneous' dynamics	Possible alternatives
'HAVE-NOTS'	• Underestimation of own power: feelings of helplessness, apathy and dependence; disorganization, internal power-struggles (can be very long-lasting!)	• Build up own organization, develop own resources. • Develop specific proposals about own needs and interests.
	• Overestimation of the reasonableness of the haves. • Contacts with haves provoke moral indignation and agression. A fighting spirit emerges which often results in provocative and violent behaviour. Possibly also in better organization and more leadership.	• Be prepared for unreasonable superior behaviour during meetings: ○ specific suggestions for ground-rules; ○ a statement of the negative consequences of sticking to the status quo; ○ an expression of own power: f.i. demonstration, harassment, etc.
	Tunnel vision 'The only way to improve our condition is to beat up the haves. The whole system has to be torn down.' Escalation.	*Negotiations* This strategy consists of two phases: 1 Building up strength. To get a more even balance of power one has to organize a strong coalition. One sometimes has to 'fight' to prove one's power and the existing interdependencies. 2 Negotiations. Develop specific proposals and a flexible negotiation strategy.

A two-day workshop on negotiating

All the materials needed for this workshop are available in appendix 2. The outline programme that follows is a working model. The appendix provides enough material to allow for adaptation to the particular experiences and preferences of participants.

This programme is of the nature of a crash course: it takes two days, including the first evening.

OBJECTIVES FOR PARTICIPANTS

1 To master a comprehensive framework of negotiating which orders important negotiating tactics.
2 To understand and to practise specific effective negotiating strategies.
3 To reach a better understanding of one's own negotiating style.
4 To understand and to practise the skills of mediation and chairmanship.

MAIN TOPICS

- Basic dimensions of negotiating:
  ○ obtaining substantial results;
  ○ promoting a constructive climate;
  ○ persuasion and authority;
  ○ creativity and flexibility.
- Profiles of the most effective combinations of specific tactics.
- The handling of stress and emotions.
- Stages in negotiation processes.
- Functions of deadlock, how to handle deadlock.
- Personal negotiating styles: effective and ineffective aspects of each style.
- Chairmanship and mediation: structure of the process, important tactics.
- Escalating factors: interventions and solutions.

PROGRAMME

First day   Presentation of programme
Mini-exercise 1
Lecture on 'The cooperation–fighting dilemma'
Short questionnaire (questionnaire 1 or 2)
Group discussion

Short lecture on 'The exploring–avoiding dilemma'
Mini-exercise 2
Evaluation form 1*

Lecture on 'Handling power and dependency'
Mini-exercise 3
Evaluation form 2

Lecture on 'Negotiating styles'
Summary 1 on personal negotiating styles

Lecture on 'Negotiating profiles'**
Simulation 1: the real estate exercise
Evaluation form 3

---

  * The evaluation forms are to be discussed by the negotiating teams after all negotiators have scored their own behaviour and that of the others involved in the exercise.
  ** See 8.3 pp. 63–7.

Second day Overview of first day, summary of major points learned, sharing of personal experiences

Introduction on 'Chairmanship and mediation'
Simulation 2: The London company exercise; evaluation
Summary 3: the chairman's role.

'Decision-making and negotiating inside organizations: escalating factors and solutions'
Mini-exercise 4 and lecture, with Summary 2 on co-operation, negotiation and fighting.

Summary and evaluation

SUPPLEMENTARY READING

Three chapters in this book summarize the outline of the programme and provide more extensive information.

1 Negotiating effectively (chapter 8). A model is described which provides negotiators with an understanding of the negotiating process. It provides an overview of important negotiating techniques. Some particularly effective strategies are described.

2 The negotiating grid (chapter 13). Two basic aspects of negotiating are combined into a grid which clarifies four personal negotiating styles: (1) analytical/aggressive; (2) flexible/aggressive; (3) ethical; (4) jovial. The main characteristics of each style are given. Clues are also provided about how to negotiate when confronted with a particular style.

3 Chairing negotiations (chapter 10). Decision-making processes about the allocation of scarce resources, such as budgets, responsibilities and office space, tend to be negotiating processes. A highly operational strategy and a check-list with procedural suggestions are provided to preside over this type of decision-making. The skills described are effective tools in resolving disputes and in mediating between different interests.

Bibliography

This bibliography should be consulted in conjunction with the literature introduced in Appendix 1.

Blake, R. and Mouton, J. (1969), *Building a Dynamic Corporation through Grid Organizational Development* (Reading, Mass., Addison-Wesley).

Bomers, G. B. J. and Peterson, R. B. (eds) (1982), *Conflict Management and Industrial Relations* (The Hague, Kluwer/Nijhoff).

Deutsch, M. (1973), *The Resolution of Conflict* (New Haven, Yale University Press).

Glasl, F. (1980), *Konfliktmanagement: Diagnose und Behandlung von Konflikten in Organisationen* (Berne, Haputverlag).

Horney, K. (1945), *Our Inner Conflicts: A Constructive Theory of Neurosis* (New York, Norton).

Mastenbroek, W. F. G. (1987), *Conflict Management and Organizational Development* (Chichester/New York, Wiley).

Mastenbroek, W. F. G. (1988), 'A Dynamic Concept of Revitalization', *Organizational Dynamics*, Spring.

Ouchi, W. G. (1981), *Theory Z: How American Business can Meet the Japanese Challenge* (Reading, Mass., Addison-Wesley).

Pascale, R. T. and Athos, A. G. (1981), *The Art of Japanese Management* (New York, Simon & Schuster).

Peters, J. and Waterman, R. H. (1982), *In Search of Excellence: Lessons from America's Best-run Companies* (New York, Harper & Row).

Pruitt, D. G. and Lewis, S. A. (1975), 'Development of Integrative
Solutions in Bilateral Negotiation' in *Journal of Personality and
Social Psychology*, 31:621–33.

Pruitt, D. G. and Lewis, S. A. (1977), 'The Psychology of Integrative
Bargaining' in D. Druckman (ed.), *Negotiations, Social Psychological Perspectives* (London, Sage).

Schulz, J. W. and Pruitt, D. G. (1978), 'The Effects of Mutual Concern on Joint Welfare' in *Journal of Experimental Social Psychology*, 14:480–91.

Schutz, W. C. (1958), *FIRO: A Three-dimensional Theory of Interpersonal Behavior* (New York, Rinehart).

Thomas, K. W. (1976), 'Conflict and Conflict Management' in
D. Dunnette (ed.), *Handbook of Industrial and Organizational
Psychology* (Chicago, Rand McNally).

Van de Vliert, E. (1984), 'Conflict: Prevention and Escalation' in
Dreenth et al. (eds), *Handbook of Work and Organizational
Psychology* (Chichester/New York, Wiley).

Walton, R. E. (1972), 'Interorganizational Decision Making and
Identity Conflict' in M. Tuite, R. Chisholm and M. Radnor (eds),
Interorganizational Decision Making (Chicago, Aldine).

Zaleznik, A. and Kets de Vries, M. F. R. (1975), *Power and the
Corporate Mind* (Boston, Houghton Mifflin).